Simply Living

Simply Living

Modern Wisdom from the Ancient Book of Proverbs

CECIL MURPHEY

Westminster John Knox Press
Louisville, Kentucky

Book design by Sharon Adams
Cover design by Lisa Buckley

First edition

Published by Westminster John Knox Press
Louisville, Kentucky

This book is printed on acid-free paper that meets the American
National Standards Institute Z39.48 standard. ♾

PRINTED IN THE UNITED STATES OF AMERICA

01 02 03 04 05 06 07 08 09 10 — 10 9 8 7 6 5 4 3 2 1

Library of Congress Cataloging-in-Publication Data is on file
at the Library of Congress, Washington, D.C.

ISBN 0-664-22267-6

Special thanks to my agent, Deidre Knight,
who suggested that I write this book;
to Nick Street of Westminster John Knox Press
for his immediate acceptance;
to the Bible Discovery class
for their ongoing encouragement;
but most of all,
my love and thanks to Shirley.

CONTENTS

Introduction

The proverbs of Solomon son of David, king of Israel:
for attaining wisdom and discipline; for understanding
words of insight; for acquiring a disciplined and prudent
life, doing what is right and just and fair . . .

Proverbs 1:1–3, NIV

"What does life mean anyway?"

"I need guidance. I wish I could figure out what God really wants me to do."

"I have dreams and goals, but my life feels empty. Insignificant. I wonder if it's worth all the stress."

"Sometimes, like at 2:30 in the morning, I wake up and wonder if life will ever get better."

"What's the value in living godly lives when those around us cheat, deceive, and work underhandedly?"

"What difference does it make to read and obey God's laws?"

These are the kinds of questions we ask today. Most of us act as if we've invented them for our generation. Yet they're surprisingly ancient questions.

One way to see how timeless the questions are—and the answers—is to read the ancient book of Proverbs. Its collection of wise sayings pondered the situations people faced in those ancient and far-off times. The thirty-one chapters in this book offer practical—and *practical* is the key word—advice and solutions to the timeless human dilemmas. Proverbs, then, is a book about how to get the most out of our relationships with God and with others.

After saying that, however, I want to point out that Proverbs is also the most secular book of the Bible! Those who seek heavy theological pronouncements might be disappointed by these simple-but-profound sayings. Proverbs makes no references to great miracles and mentions no covenants, nor does it try to picture divine redemption. No prophet shouts, "Thus saith the Lord." It ignores not only the grand themes, but also the history of Abraham and Israel and the Exodus and the wilderness wanderings.

Instead of being a chronicle of gallant deeds, Proverbs focuses on people who don't perform heroic acts or change the course of history. The practical-look-at-life sayings refer to the problems faced by human beings throughout history. The bits of wisdom in its pages, once understood, are as pragmatic and meaningful today as they were 3,000 years ago. The approach says, "This is the way to live happily in the world."

Proverbs concentrates on the human search for meaning. Through reason, experience, thoughts, common sense, and elementary scientific observations, the writer seeks to discover God in the details of daily life. The topics sound remarkably like the kinds of problems and situations we face today.

This Old Testament book refers to the sagacity and the folly of ordinary people. We read a wide range of admonitions against gossip, talking too much, defrauding others, gluttony, and sexual temptations. We receive instructions for raising our children, warnings against being influenced by the wrong crowd, and pleas to avoid unscrupulous business dealings. We even have a few references to table manners.

Traditionally, authorship has been ascribed to King Solomon. According to 1 Kings 4:29–34, this brilliant man composed 3,000 proverbs, so tradition may be right, but most contemporary scholars agree it is simply a collection of folk wisdom from ancient times. Consequently, I'll refer to the sages or wise ones as authors of this book.

The purpose of Proverbs, as we learn in its first chapter, was to educate people in the ways of good and wise living. Scholars think this compilation may have been intended as a textbook for the sons of the nobility, the wealthy, or the already well educated in Israel hundreds of years before the birth of Jesus. The sages were teachers who taught others to live uprightly within their society.

Now, centuries later, the audience has changed, but the principles haven't; the writers and collectors produced a book filled with enduring wisdom and common sense. Despite being an ancient book, Proverbs reads remarkably well today. That is, if we are willing to search for meaning behind the literal words. Often, because of differences in culture and lifestyle, this meaning may not be immediately apparent. But the wisdom is there, thrown out in a seemingly random manner, often with no seeming connection to the instructions before or after.

My purpose here is to try to lift the veil that separates ancient lives from our own. By understanding how our forebears coped with abiding human dilemmas, we might be able to adapt their hard-won wisdom to the problems we face in our increasingly technological age.

To understand Proverbs, we need first to recognize its patterns. The basic form of Proverbs, called a *mashal,* consists of two parallel lines in the Hebrew text, a structure that isn't always apparent in English. Often the second line is *synonymous* with the first—that is, the second repeats the same idea in different words. The other form, called an *antithetical,* points out a contrast. Whichever form it takes, each couplet makes a single point.

Second, we need to recognize that the teachings are a practical guide in life. Unlike the Ten Commandments, which legislate behavior using "You shall" and "You shall not," Proverbs tries a more subtle method. The laws are there—but offered in a way that allows readers to uncover the truths for themselves. The emphasis falls on human responsibility rather than obedience to God's specific commands.

Third, we should note that the preferred name for God is LORD—written in small capital letters. This is the method translators traditionally use to let us know that the word in the Hebrew text is Yahweh (or Jehovah). I note this because Yahweh was the divine covenant name—the name given exclusively to the people of Israel. It's strange that Yahweh appears, because the references to God in Proverbs have an almost irreligious quality about them, as if they refer to the moral and ethical laws of the universe. Today I hear secular people talking in the same vein and using such terms as "the

Cosmos." Maybe the wise ones used LORD as a way of hinting at the divine imperatives implicit in the workaday wisdom of daily life. Anyone can read Proverbs and benefit from the experience. Those who derive the most benefit will understand that this is a greater wisdom, spoken through the sages.

On a personal note, I have to confess that I'm intrigued by the general optimism of Proverbs. Many biblical texts emphasize human failure. Despite a few dark sayings, Proverbs offers the possibility of our achieving the better goals of life. It holds out the prospect of contentment and happiness for readers who grow in wisdom. In effect, Proverbs says, "Learn the laws, obey them, and you will be rewarded and enlightened."

We do have to put a little effort into our study of these sayings. Most of the time, if we read the words and ask, "What's the *principle* involved?" we're getting close to what the sages want us to learn.

One of the challenges in studying Proverbs is that there is no logical arrangement to the verses. Various scholars have attempted to make artificial arrangements. My solution is to divide the wise sayings into four categories, although I could just as easily have made eight or twelve. I've chosen four categories and given samples of sayings from each of them:

1. Living with God
2. Living with the Family
3. Living and Working with Others
4. Living with Business and Law

As I've said above, cultural situations have changed, but the principles behind ethical and honorable living remain. In short, Proverbs is a book of ancient wisdom whose principles shine forth just as strongly today.

Modern Proverb: By doing what's right, we gain understanding and live a contented life.

PART ONE

Living with God

Pondering Proverbs

The proverbs of Solomon . . . for learning about wisdom and instruction, for understanding words of insight, for gaining instruction in wise dealings, righteousness, justice, and equity . . .

Proverbs 1:1–3

"How did he know to do that?" I've asked that question every time I've pondered the story of the two women arguing over who was the mother of a newborn baby.

Recorded in 1 Kings 3:16–28, the story centers on two prostitutes who apparently lived together and who both had newborns. In the middle of the night, one infant died and the mother switched hers for the live baby. In the morning, the second mother thought her child was dead, but then she realized the deception. They argued over the infant.

They brought the case before King Solomon, and most people know what the wise king did: " 'Bring me a sword,' and they brought a sword before the king. The king said, 'Divide the living boy in two; then give half to the one, and half to the other' " (1 Kings 3:24–25).

"But the woman whose son was alive said to the king— because compassion for her son burned within her—'Please, my lord, give her the living boy; certainly do not kill him' " (v. 26a).

The other woman said, "It shall be neither mine nor yours; divide it" (v. 26b).

That's where the wisdom of Solomon shone, because he said, "Give the first woman the living boy; do not kill him. She is his mother" (v. 27).

My immediate question has always been "How did Solomon know to do that?" What if both women had objected? Or both had said, "Yes, kill the baby"? I wouldn't have known what to

7

do. If I had been the ruler, I probably would have set up some kind of court of inquiry and gone through elaborate steps to determine the true identity.

Solomon perceived the answer instantly. That's called wisdom—knowing what to do and how to do it at exactly the right moment.

That's the kind of wisdom we read in verse after verse of this powerful book of Proverbs. And it isn't even what we'd call a spiritual book. God is referred to many times, but secularized people could just as easily substitute "Higher Power" or some other such word and the wisdom would come out the same.

Let's try a contrast. If we read the prophets, their basic message comes down to one word: *return*. Return to God. Leave your sins, cheating, lying, stealing, and worshiping false gods. That kind of behavior. If we read the letters of the New Testament, the key word is *therefore*. The writers point to Jesus Christ, his death and resurrection, and say, "Jesus died for us; *therefore,* this is the way we need to live."

So why should we ponder Proverbs? The book is roughly 3,000 years old, and we've come a long way in scientific knowledge and technology since then. Why ponder the ancient sayings of a less-enlightened age?

Perhaps that's just the point. They had less technology. The wise were the curious, the observers, the ones who scrutinized the actions of others. Despite the centuries between them and us, they understood the workings of the human heart. They hadn't invented such terms as the *ego* and *id, shadow side,* or *selfhood,* but they understood human motivation and desires. Proverbs could be cut out of the pages of the Bible and used as a textbook for getting along in the world.

When I started to ponder the book of Proverbs, I felt overwhelmed by the number of words linked with wisdom. It took me a long time to realize that the words, phrases, concepts, and ideas overlap. The book offers many directions to follow, but we can sum it up in one sentence: We study Proverbs to become wiser than we are now.

Initially, I made the mistake of trying to figure out every

word and the nuances of those words, and I soon became lost. Once I realized that this is *practical* wisdom, or even secular wisdom, then I realized it's a book filled with pithy sayings on how to live happily and healthily in this world.

Proverbs contains material for living in the world, for living with other people, for our conduct in the workplace. It's the book that tells us the wise things to do if we want the best kind of life.

The Hebrew word for wisdom is difficult to explain, although it's not a complex word. In fact, in tune with the melody of the entire book, it's a practical term.

For example, when Moses and the Israelites began to build the Tabernacle in the wilderness—a kind of temple-tent—they chose the most talented workers to oversee it. Moses called out Bezalel because "he has filled him . . . with divine spirit, with skill, intelligence, and knowledge in every kind of craft, to devise artistic designs, to work in gold, silver, and bronze . . . He has filled them with skill . . . " (Exodus 35:30–32, 35). The phrase "with skill" is the word *chokmah*, a word usually translated as *wisdom*, which is how the NKJV translates it. Actually, the word means technical knowledge or the know-how and skill to do a good job. One version translates it as *ability*. In Ezekiel 27:8, *chokmah* refers to sailors, and most translators use *skilled* there.

The simplest meaning of the word, then, is the skill to cope with the practical. In Proverbs, this ability to do the best we're capable of in life is called wisdom. If we want harmony and success, we need to "know" wisdom; that is, to have the ability to make our lives successful.

Modern Proverb: *Ponder the wisdom of the ancient proverbs. The writers understood human problems. To ponder their words makes us wiser.*

Fearing God

The fear of the LORD is the beginning of knowledge; fools despise wisdom and instruction.

Proverbs 1:7

Wayne had one of the sharpest minds I'd ever encountered. Not only did he know a great deal about any topic, but his quick, penetrating insights constantly impressed me. Wayne called himself an agnostic and used the cliché "If there is a god, I don't bother him and he doesn't bother me."

Although I admired Wayne, I finally said to him one day, "I can't figure you out. How can you not believe in God and yet understand so much about the world? Why, just the orderliness of the seasons and—"

"Listen, if I started to think about God, I'd have to make changes in my life and it's easier to live this way."

He laughed, but I knew Wayne meant what he said. He preferred to rely on his brilliance instead of allowing God to invade his world or seriously contemplating that there was any power beyond himself. Wayne isn't alone. I regularly meet what I call *practical agnostics*—those who claim belief in God but rarely show any evidence of a relationship to the Creator of all things.

Wayne missed the whole point of life; so do the practical agnostics. I sometimes wonder how they make any sense out of life without some awareness of a creator or even a higher being. Proverbs tells us that the fear of God is where life starts. I understand agnostics—when I was a teenager I decided I was one. I wasn't sure that God existed and if he did, I reasoned, I saw no need for him. My busy life pushed God out of the picture—if God existed. "I can handle whatever comes my way," I said.

When someone asked me about God, I recall saying, "I think dumb kids and old people probably need something like that to believe in. Kids like Santa Claus, right? So why not God? And old people need something to take their minds off dying."

Then I faced the realities of my life. A time came when I couldn't figure out things for myself—a time when life didn't make sense. When I was about 21, my world turned meaningless and my existence seemed empty.

Is this all there is to life?

I must have asked that question a hundred times before I started to seek answers. I read books, asked questions, and talked to the most brilliant people I knew. Nothing helped much. Then I realized—and I can't begin to explain how—that I had to give God a chance. I had met many believers.

What if they're right?

For maybe a week that question wouldn't leave me. So I did the only sensible thing I could think of—I turned to God. "If you're real," I prayed, "show me. Help me understand you."

As I wrote the words above, I thought of some of my friends who scorned such talk. "God is for those who are too weak to handle their own lives," said one of my co-workers. For other friends, reliance on God meant being weak and needing a crutch, as I had once felt. They said those things condescendingly or arrogantly, but I think they had it exactly right!

God *is* a crutch.

God is a helper—a lifter-up of the depressed, a strengthener of the weak. God becomes the "edge," the boost we need to leap over the next hurdle, the strengthening voice to push us onward when we're ready to quit.

If I understand the meaning of Proverbs 1:7—which is really like the heading for the entire book—the writer means this: Start with God. If you start right, you end up right. If you start with your own wisdom or insight, it's not only useless, but it will lead you to a dead end.

By the way, *fear* is better translated as *awe* or *reverence*. I like to think of it simply as taking God into account when we cope with life's situations. Reverence for God is another way to admit our human limitation. Awe of God says, "I can only go so far, and then I need help—a help stronger than I and a power I can't manufacture."

Isn't it rather arrogant to think that anyone can truly make it through life without relying on outside help? Nobody ever makes it in life alone. All of us need help. I've never read a success story in which there wasn't at least one person—a teacher, friend, or relative—who didn't figure into the victory saga. That's the way life is, and I believe we're made to depend on other people.

Then why stop with the help of another human when there is an even greater power available? Isn't it just possible that our dependence on other humans is a way to reflect our need to rely on God? Anytime in life, beginning with infancy, we can't survive without human hands embracing us. What if God arranged for such relationships to point us heavenward?

Those are the thoughts I played with in the early days of opening myself to Yahweh. Part of the reverence came from reasoning and analogy. But mostly, it came from my acute sense of need.

Needy I was . . .

And needy I've remained.

"The fear of the Lord is the beginning of knowledge; fools despise wisdom and instruction." This proverb emphasizes two sides of a picture. First is the reverence for God. But it's more than acknowledging the Creator of the world. It views the contrast between Yahweh—the one who is totally different from the created—and ourselves. When we grasp that concept, it pushes us toward the kind of awe the proverb advocates.

Like young children, we're often too arrogant to realize that we need help. We're too often like the two-year-old child who insists, "I can put my shoes on myself," but we can't do it, no matter how hard we try.

I wonder how Moses felt the time God appeared to him. In those days, Moses, who forty years earlier had murdered an Egyptian and had fled from the Egyptian palace, had become a shepherd. The assumption is that God didn't play any significant role in his life until one day his life changed forever. While tending his sheep, Moses spotted a bush that, although on fire, wasn't consumed. As the man crept toward the amazing sight, he heard a voice: "Take off your shoes. You're on holy ground."

Or how did Paul feel during the first moments of his encounter with the Divine? Paul was a zealous Pharisee, out to do whatever was necessary to stop the spread of the message of salvation through Jesus Christ. On the way to the city of Damascus, he was struck down and remained blind for three days until God sent a believer named Ananias to pray for him.

What about the young man at Nain who had died, and in answer to his mother's plea, Jesus touched him and brought him back to life? I wonder how he felt about life and the One who gives it.

What about the parting of the water of the Red Sea? Or the parting of the Jordan when the people crossed it to enter the Promised Land? What kind of responses did such events evoke among those who had been indifferent or unsure about the reality of Yahweh?

Most of us don't have the awe-filled experiences those ancient people did. We have a written record called the Bible; we also have recorded experiences of people through the centuries who have felt the touch of the Divine in their lives. We make ourselves candidates to experience that same touch when we open our minds enough to say, "God is greater and more powerful than I am."

There's another side to this proverb: What does it mean to fear or reverence God? How does it affect our lives in practical ways?

At the least, it means that if we reverence God, we'll respond by heeding divine teachings, listening to God's will, and obeying whatever guidance Yahweh offers. The Bible makes a strong presentation that our Creator, our Heavenly Parent, the All-Powerful One of the universe, acts for the benefit of the human race.

Think about what that means. More simply put, all through the Bible, the message is that God wants to do us good and seeks only the best for us. To fear Yahweh, then, implies that we will obey, as we learn the right way and follow it.

As I was writing those words, I thought of an incident with a writer-friend named Rich Stanford. An unpublished writer asked him to look over her work and make any suggestions. He read and heavily edited the manuscript. When she saw what he had done, she said, "Thank you for reading it," and walked away. The anger in her voice made Rich aware that she didn't like all the editing he had done.

Later, when Rich tried to apologize to her, she waved away his words. "I didn't like what you wrote, but I'm not stupid enough to ignore good advice—even if it's not what I wanted to hear."

Isn't that the way God works with us? Sometimes we have to hear the kind of things we don't like. We find red lights and detours along the way. Not only do we need to hear God say, "This is the way. Walk in it," but to fear God also means to hear the whisper, "This isn't the way. Turn around."

All too often, only in retrospect do we admit, "That was truly for my good." We begin with awe, and if we faithfully follow, we end up with knowledge, as the proverb says. Fear of God leads us along the path of wisdom and understanding— and that's what makes life worth living.

The fear of the Lord works quite simply. We reverence God, who in turn shows us the right way to go, and if we give heed, we learn, we mature, and we live healthier and happier lives.

When we stop to think about it, isn't that what all of us really want—just to enjoy living?

Modern Proverb: *Acknowledging God is the starting place for wisdom. Only fools reject wisdom and good advice.*

But It Hurts!

My child, do not despise the LORD's discipline or be weary of his reproof, for the LORD reproves the one he loves as a father the son in whom he delights.

Proverbs 3:11–12

Matt was one of those extra-smart kids who learned quickly and aced all the tests. But I also heard a teacher say to him once, "You don't have compassion for classmates who aren't as smart as you are. I hope you'll fail somewhere in your life."

What an odd thing to say, I thought at the time. Over the years, however, I realized the wisdom of her words. Matt was bright and quite impatient with those who couldn't keep up with his fast-propelled thinking.

Twenty years after high school, Matt and I talked, and he said he remembered the teacher's words. In fact, his initial reaction had been like mine.

"When I got into graduate school, I finally figured it out," he said, and then laughed. "Okay, I figured it out after the unthinkable happened."

Matt *failed* a test! He didn't just do badly—he pulled down the third-lowest score in the class. By then he was in his early twenties, rapidly progressing toward his doctoral degree, and had never come close to academic failure before. Although Matt admitted that he had failed in a course that just never did make sense to him, that semester he had worked more for that class than for all the others combined. Still he failed. At that particular university, he had to take two remedial classes to make up for his failure, and it was humiliating for him.

"It took me years to reach this place, but now I can tell you I'm glad I failed," he said. "I needed to bomb."

The teacher had been right, he admitted, because he had

never had much concern for those who just couldn't get it or didn't catch on as quickly as he did. Only when he himself was in such a position could he understand.

"My Heavenly Father cared enough to rub my nose in failure," Matt said. "That experience changed my life, and I slowly began to understand and care about those who weren't as bright as I was."

Yet when he first failed, he had asked, "God, why are you punishing me?" He went through a period of deep depression and intense soul-searching. Slowly, he admitted, it dawned on him that his failure was an act of grace and divine love in action.

Yet often we immediately jump to questions such as "Why me? What did I ever do to deserve this?" Isn't it amazing how failures can be understood if we think of them as being the means to provide *for our needs?*

That's the intent of this proverb. It thunders at us that failure or hardship doesn't have to be punishment. In fact, for those of us who sincerely seek God, punishment isn't the appropriate word. We need to think instead of the word *discipline.*

We're pupils of the Divine Teacher. If we don't learn what we need the easy way, God lovingly sends hardships to enable us to get it. Whenever we lumber through dark valleys of failure, we may never find satisfactory explanations for our suffering, but we can ask ourselves one question: "What can I learn from this experience?"

Matt learned compassion—gradually—and he also learned to value the brilliant mind God had given him. "You know, I am smart, but it's a gift," he said. "I feel sorry for those gifted people who don't see their talents as expressions of God's love. They often act as if they did it all by themselves."

Thinking about this particular proverb caused me to reflect on the great heroes of faith. Every one of them went through great times of testing or disciplining. In fact, I suspect that what we'd term hardship was God's school of instruction.

For example, Abraham wanted a son; he waited twenty-five years for God to give him one. Then, later, God ordered Abraham to offer his son as a sacrifice (see Genesis 22). He didn't actually sacrifice the boy, but what a test that might have been. (Offering a human sacrifice wasn't that uncommon in the culture of Abraham's day. So the testing wasn't as bizarre as it may sound.)

Consider David. Even though promised the kingship, for years he fled from King Saul before David's ascension to the throne. Jeremiah lived inside dungeons and knew the torture of being plunged into the bottoms of wells for long periods. He often feared for his life. Paul's list of disciplines goes from brutal imprisonment to being stoned and left for dead. Peter received several verbal slaps from Jesus and failed the big exam after his teacher's arrest.

That's how it works—if we follow God, we can take it as a reality that we'll encounter hardship and difficulties of some kind. When we suffer, that's God's way to discipline us, and it's a necessary part of our training. "Now, discipline always seems painful rather than pleasant at the time, but later it yields the peaceful fruit of righteousness to those who have been trained by it" (Hebrews 12:11).

We can rebel, cry, reject, or hate it—and we probably do all of these at times. But once we've gone through the turmoil and traveled through dark nights of loneliness, we recognize the experience as an act of God's parental love.

The downside of this proverb reminds me of an incident I witnessed in the food court of a mall on Atlanta's south side. A man was there with his son, maybe five years old. Not only did the boy make a lot of noise, but he also threw scraps of food on the floor. "Don't like that," he said as he pulled the lettuce out of his hamburger. He did that several times and the father just kept saying, "Please don't do that."

The boy had strewn as much food on the floor as he ate, and then he demanded another hamburger.

A woman sat a few feet away from them, obviously disgusted at the behavior. She got up, and as she walked by, she shook her head. The father said, "He's not easy to handle."

"*Him?* You're the one who's disgusting. You obviously don't care or you wouldn't let him get away with it."

The man didn't reply, but he grabbed his son's arms and

pulled the screaming child from the food court. He didn't bother to clean up the floor.

That incident happened in 1983. The boy would be an adult now, and I wonder what kind of person he's turned out to be. My guess is that he's probably not a very nice person—unless Dad changed and lovingly disciplined him.

As I understand the Bible, the kindest thing that God can do for us is to say no to our selfish desires and stomp on our toes when we start walking down the wrong path.

We can resent God's loving discipline. We can grumble and get angry with God. I remember a woman named Verna who often complained about her hard life. "I think God has his picks" was the way she said it, "and I'm not one of them."

Or maybe she was one of God's favorites. Maybe God cared enough to keep at her and not allow her to go astray. However, I don't think Verna ever saw it that way.

I don't know anyone who enjoys enduring bad times or encountering hardships. However, if we understand the purpose behind them, eventually we're able to look back and say, "Thank God it happened."

I'm convinced that the hard times I've had in my life prove the constancy and love of my Heavenly Father. The suffering for me proves that parental love—and it's not a sign of displeasure. I like the way Psalm 119:71 puts it: "The suffering you sent me was good for me, for it taught me to pay attention to your principles" (NLT).

A friend once said to me, "God smiles when we're joyful, whispers when we're going down the right path, but shouts when we're going through difficulty." By shouting, he meant that if we don't heed the whisper to go in the right direction, God shouts at us through roadblocks, hardships, and suffering. At the time, it may sound harsh; but then, isn't that how discipline always seems when we're experiencing it?

Modern Proverb: *When we find problems and hardships on every side, it's not punishment but discipline by our Loving Heavenly Parent, who wants us to be perfect.*

Balanced Living

Trust in the LORD with all your heart, and do not rely on your own insight. In all your ways acknowledge him, and he will make straight your paths.

Proverbs 3:5–6

"I'm trying to balance my life," said a friend. "I want to get control over my life and not be rushing around all the time."

"I became so busy doing things that I didn't have much time to be," said a distressed friend years ago.

"I'm making enough to send my kids to the best schools, but I don't have enough time to enjoy being with them."

Do those complaints sound familiar? Most of us have been there sometime in our life, or we still may be there. For a long time I struggled to balance my life. I thought balancing your life was like using the Quicken software program: You punch in numbers, and it balances your checking account. It's a simple program. You type in the amounts from each check, let the machine do the math, and within seconds, your checkbook figures agree with the bank's.

If only life were that easily balanced.

Not long ago I began to think about that concept.

It didn't take long for me to admit to myself that I don't live a balanced life. The more I thought about my friends, the more I realized they don't either. In fact, they fight over the same issues I do. Then I asked myself, "Do I really want to live a balanced life?"

"I'm not sure I do," my own voice answered. "Think about it. Doesn't balanced living sound bland, boring, and uneventful?"

Then a new idea struck me. Yes, it can be that or it can be a life of constant, unrelenting stress. That brought up a second visual image. Years ago on TV, I watched a man juggle five oranges while talking to the audience. The talented can do it, but what enormous energy and concentration it demands to keep all five pieces moving at the same time.

Okay, I know that when most people talk about balance, they mean they want to slow down, to give a little more time to the important things, and either to push away time-wasting demands or to avoid activities they dislike doing. They're serious about wanting unencumbered lives, but they rarely turn that desire into reality.

That desire reminds me of a conversation I had years ago with Skip and Suzy Cothran. A successful salesman, Skip listed his hectic schedule for the next three weeks. He decried not having enough time for his family and for church activities. "After I get over that next big hill," he said, "I can relax a little and get my life back into balance."

Suzy laughed. "No, after that, you'll start getting busy all over again."

She was right. Skip knew it and so did I. He talked and he wished, but he didn't know how to stop the busy schedule from controlling his life. He also began to make changes so that he wasn't always putting everything into "that next big hill."

Remembering those insightful words from Suzy started some deep thinking for me. Too many of us fill our hours with many events and activities—which we agree to involve ourselves in—then we complain because we can't figure out how to get twenty-eight hours of living out of only twenty-four. We tell ourselves that if we could only figure out how to free ourselves of things we don't really want to do, we could concentrate on what we really want. All too often, however, we make the big, big mistake of piling on activities so that we can get them over with and think we'll have more free time when we finish. It's not long before we've overloaded ourselves again. Does this sound familiar?

That pattern has been the story of most of my life.

That's also the story of our modern culture. Or at least that's the way many of my friends try to cope with life. Maybe it's because, for most of us, it's a compulsion to fill every waking moment with doing or achieving. No matter how many computers and cell phones we have, there's never enough time to get everything done.

Unless we're forced to quit work, most of us won't get rid of our business opportunities. Even then, we'll find a hundred other indispensable activities to consume our energies and keep the clock ticking. So we'll continue to struggle to compact our schedules, get more things done in less time, until we finally attain balance. Why not? Haven't we been told we can have it all?

Can we? Or do we need "it all"?

We can vary our approach and ask a different question: "Can I ever balance my life?"

The answer is simple: "No, we can't." In our fast-paced culture, who can possibly get everything? If we push away the unimportant, delegate the insignificant, and concentrate on the urgent, the juggling doesn't stop. Most of us operate our lives the way Skip used to. We find new interests and attractions to add to an already overloaded life, and we smile and say to ourselves, "It's only another two hours a week for six weeks." Then we're back where we started.

Let's face reality. We don't find that perfect balance because moving toward balance isn't the answer. While we groan, mumble, complain, and keep packing more commitments into our schedules, most of us are doing something that's inherently wrong.

We're stealing.

We're stealing time from the important and giving in to the urgent or insistent. Stealing to accomplish everything also involves something even more important than giving in to the urgent. Too many of us have figured how to get more things done in a single day. All we have to do is steal an hour or two from our normal sleep needs. Experts, surveys, and long-term studies regularly inform us that at least one-third of Americans live in a sleep-deprived state. That is, although our divinely fashioned bodies need seven to eight hours of sleep, we force ourselves to get by on six. Or five.

What we don't reckon with, of course, is that thieves eventually get caught. We're stealing our health. And eventually, justice prevails. I can relate this from personal experience.

We need those seven to eight hours of sleep because that's when our immune system goes to work and does its daily repair by erasing stress and relaxing overworked bodies and preparing us for the next day. If we don't give our immune systems the needed repair time, our bodies fight back. It may be a simple cold, an acidic stomach, or an allergic reaction. Over time, it can become serious. We can't keep stealing and get away with it forever.

For example, for nearly twenty years, I existed on five hours of sleep. "Who needs more than that?" I used to boast. Of course, one day my body rebelled and I ended up with an ulcer and a three-day stay in the hospital. Lying flat on my back forced me to reflect on my life. I promised God I would make changes, and one of them was to learn to take care of my body. After all, the Bible says that the body is God's holy temple (as in Romans 12:1; 1 Corinthians 3:16; 1 Corinthians 6:19–20). For the past two decades, I've been honoring God's temple and keeping it healthy.

We know that all machines need downtime if they are to function at their best—time to turn off the engines and to do maintenance. Our bodies are no different. Isn't it time, then, to admit that balance is not the ideal? Instead of trying to balance everything we want in life, maybe we need to push away a few things.

Perhaps *focus* says it better than any other word. A focused life faces what comes, but doesn't get distracted or distraught over not packing in all those extra activities. A focused life chooses priorities and loyalties and pushes away those demands that distract and lead away from our primary objectives.

To live a focused life, we have to make decisions. We admit there are opportunities and activities—desirable projects or fun events—we're not going to fit into our lives. And that means making choices. Sometimes we need to choose, not between good and bad, but between the good and the best.

Or try it this way: We need to focus on what's best for us.

And how do we know what's best?

Proverbs 3:5–6 presents the principle of focus: "Trust in the LORD with all your heart, and do not rely on your own insight.

In all your ways acknowledge him, and he will make straight your paths."

This proverb is written in the form of Hebrew poetry. The two statements of verse 5 intend to say the same thing in a different form: Trust God. If we do that, we don't rely on our brilliance, our time-saving methods, or our uptight schedule. We trust in a superior wisdom—a Supreme Power—Yahweh—who knows what's best for us.

To begin to live the full lives we yearn for—the lives that get us excitedly out of bed every morning and eager for the day—isn't it time that we trusted in some more objective guide than ourselves? Isn't it at least possible that the Creator who made us might also be the Guide who willingly leads and the Provider who lovingly cares for us?

This proverb teaches us that when we focus in the right direction and lean toward the God who created us and loves us, we can expect a happier, more fulfilled life. It won't ever be balanced, but it can be peacefully focused.

Modern Proverb: *If we rely on God's guidance, we'll live a focused, more contented life, and that means a happier life.*

Just Commit!

Commit your work to the LORD, and then your plans will succeed.

Proverbs 16:3, NLT

What a thrilling promise! What a wonderful way for people to live! We commit our work to God, and then we can rest assured that all will go well for us. That's what the text says.

Of course, we always have to haggle over words, so we struggle over what it means to commit and what the writer meant by "will succeed." (Some versions read "will be established," but the meaning is the same.) Even so, it sounds rather simple.

Then why do I have so much trouble making business choices? Choosing friends? Deciding which activities to participate in? Deciding on my future career?

The simplest way for some to interpret this proverb may be to pray this way: "I've applied for a position on the next rung up. I'm your follower and want to do this to serve you better." We may not add, but we certainly imply, "Therefore, I know you'll give me the promotion."

It might work that way. But what happens if it doesn't? How do we react if all our plans for advancement fail? Or if we get fired instead?

Could it be that the problem is the approach we take?

Or maybe we need to reconsider commitment. Think of it this way: We figure out what we want, tell God, commit ourselves to God, and—

There! That's it.

We're already off the narrow path. For most of us, it's a matter of adding one step between "figure out what we want"

24

and "tell God." It's human to think and act that way, and probably all of us do it at times. But it's also the way that eventually traps us.

Let's try it another way. We live in a culture that values control. We admire self-control and self-discipline. We esteem those who take charge during tense situations and remain firm. We applaud those who tell of their battles losing weight or getting the right job. Often they tell us about the valleys and begin their turnaround and success with "Then I took control of my life."

We love the power of those statements and vicariously rejoice with them. Yet if we follow the same path they did, we may be marching in the wrong direction. We forget one of the Bible's basic principles—and one that's made clear in this proverb.

We begin with that illusive quality we call God's will.

Probably all of us recognize the need to align ourselves with God's will. We may not be clear about the divine will—and that's where the problems come. Too often we assume we're walking down the right path because it's prudent and sensible.

Maybe it is. But what if it isn't?

Perhaps my story will help. In my second year of seminary, my life was going well. At seminary I hovered right at the academic top and knew I'd receive a generous scholarship if I kept up my grades. Another organization had provided financial help for me and assured me they would continue. Another eighteen months and I'd have my master's degree in theology. I had a master's in education and had taught in both public and private schools. It seemed as if the logical career move would be for me to enter a doctoral program, earn my Ph.D., and then teach on a college or seminary level. My friends agreed with me; my professors encouraged me; my wife said it made sense. Everything indicated that it was the prudent thing to do.

Even though I prayed about it often, I don't think I ever had serious questions about whether it was the right choice. More than once I committed my plans to God by praying like this: "God, I believe this is right, so . . ."

Then I came to a bend in the road, and everything changed.

In the middle of my second year in seminary, I got a frantic telephone call from the dean of students. A small, local church needed a preacher the next day and their regular supply preacher had a death in the family. The dean had gone down the list of seniors and none was available. Then he started alphabetically down the middler list. My name is Murphey, and I was the fourteenth person he called from my class.

"Of course," I said. "I can do that."

The next day I preached, and I don't think I delivered any extraordinary sermon. Yet something happened to me—something over which I had no control nor had ever considered before. When I stood behind that pulpit and stared into the faces of perhaps twenty-five people, most of them elderly, I felt I belonged there. My sermon connected with those people, and in my heart, I sensed they listened and responded.

Becoming a pastor had not been an option for me. I was a teacher, so it just wasn't anything to pray seriously about.

At the end of the worship service, five people gathered in a corner, and I could hear them talking quietly, but I didn't pay much attention. After a few minutes, all of them came up to me. "Would you consider being our supply pastor as long as you're in seminary?" one of them asked.

To shorten the story, I said yes, and I received permission from the seminary on the condition that I kept up my grades. (I kept them up.) For the next eighteen months, I became their pastor. The church flourished and the attendance more than doubled. Finally, I finished my seminary training and was ready to graduate, and I had been accepted by a major university for its doctoral program.

I started my Ph.D. course and finished the first year's courses. About a week before the end of the year, I was hospitalized with ulcers. For three days I lay in a hospital bed, although I didn't require surgery. That time confined to a bed forced me to examine my life. I couldn't figure out what was going on. I admitted to myself I wasn't enjoying my life very much, and for the first time, I had to push myself to study.

On the morning of the second day, I prayed, "God, help me understand what's happening." I had hardly said those words when a shocking realization filled my brain. "No!" I yelled to the sterile hospital room. "This can't be."

In that electric moment, I realized something: I had committed my work to God—but it was the work *I* had chosen. I hadn't allowed God to choose the divine path for me. It wasn't an act of deliberate disobedience, but one of just not opening all the doors.

"I can't help it. I'm hooked," I told my wife later. "I want to be a pastor." I could hardly believe the words I said, but they were true. For months, she had sensed that's where I belonged but had waited for me to realize it.

I dropped out of graduate school. For the next fourteen years, being a pastor became the focus of my life. To my amazement, I didn't miss having dropped out of the academic world. In fact, almost every morning when I went to church, I paused to thank God for calling me to that work.

I don't think I'm that unusual. Probably most people end up in a different place in their occupations and relationships than they ever imagined. Committing our way to God means being open—fully open—to wherever God directs. Our commitment gives God the opportunity to steer us to the right paths.

For me, God took charge when I surrendered control of my plans and dreams. That is, once I committed my work to Yahweh, my preferences and desires no longer mattered. Once I realized that my plans were just that—my plans, and not the guidance of Yahweh—it wasn't difficult to surrender.

Surrender brings joy and peace. The day I withdrew from my doctoral program was one of the happiest days of my life.

I also learned a valuable lesson about commitment. It's really simple: When I'm doing the work God has planned for me, I have an inner contentment. No matter how many problems hit me, I know I will succeed, because I'm assured that I'm doing the right thing.

Modern Proverb: *If we allow God to direct our lives, we do the right thing that brings us happiness.*

Despising Ourselves

Those who ignore instruction despise themselves, but those who heed admonition gain understanding.
Proverbs 15:32

I don't suppose I'll ever forget Bernie, although I haven't seen him for fifteen years. I had formed a writing group for five ministers, all of whom expressed a desire to write and publish. They were all seminary-educated, with years of practical experience behind them.

Because I was already publishing regularly, I offered to teach them what I knew about the craft. Long before Internet days, we decided that a week before each meeting, each person would mail the rest of us a copy of his manuscript; we would edit immediately, and then we'd discuss the writing when we came together.

I'll say this much about Bernie: He never failed to produce an article. We made dozens of marks and notations on our copies, explained our reasons, and returned the article to him. By mutual agreement, each person took the edited pages home, read over our suggestions, and made whatever corrections he felt were necessary. He then prepared to mail out the revised article for the next meeting.

For eleven months, Bernie didn't miss a single meeting of what we called the Scriptiques. Yes, he made changes—that is, he always made punctuation corrections. Once or twice, he'd change a verb, but he just wouldn't make any significant alterations.

When Tom, Ed, Hugh, or I explained why something didn't sound right or showed him how to make a sentence clearer, Bernie never disagreed. Usually he nodded and said, "I'll work on it." But he didn't make those changes.

More than once I'd ask, "Do you understand what I mean?"

"Oh, yes, I do," he'd say. But that didn't result in any changes in the paper he presented at the next meeting.

One time when I pointed out that his excessive use of passive verbs weakened the writing, he said, "I like using passive verbs." I had already spent fifteen minutes explaining one of the basic principles of writing.

Bernie said he heard, but his response closed the discussion. So what do these responses say about Bernie? He heard *the words* of instruction, but he never did anything about what he heard. He kept saying he understood, so why didn't such changes show in his manuscripts?

From a biblical perspective, he did not "hear" us. In the Old Testament, to hear implies a responsive action. Quite simply, those who hear God speak, obey.

It took me several months before I figured Bernie out. He couldn't handle our corrections and fought against any implication that his writing needed help. To make the kind of changes we suggested signaled messages to him that he wasn't ready to receive.

I think Proverbs 15:32 helps explain Bernie. This verse says that those who ignore the help offered despise *themselves.* Quite an interesting perspective, because we don't usually think of it that way.

Instead, we assume they despise the dispensers of knowledge. "You don't know what you're talking about" is one way they reply, and that implies they despise the speaker. Their attitude says to us, "You think you know so much and that you're better than anyone else. Well, you don't know anything."

Too often they're like Bernie. It took me a long time to figure out why he wouldn't make corrections. *He couldn't.* Deep within, Bernie was too fragile to follow what we urged. If I had suggested that Bernie change two words in an article, I think he might have handled that without a serious problem. The corrections the group mentioned were major. He had violated the rules of the craft; he didn't understand the need for past-perfect tense; and writing dialogue overwhelmed him. His worst problem was his refusal to write in a logical flow.

"You need to go from A to B to C to D," Tom told him several times. "This looks like A to R to D to F to G."

"Makes sense to me," Bernie said.

Without trying to judge the man, my way of looking at him is to say that, in his fragility, he had to justify his article to himself. If he didn't, then he'd have been a fool not to accept our changes. But making those changes would say to him, "Bernie, you're one terrible writer. You're a failure. You don't know what you're doing."

None of us ever said anything unkind to him; in fact, we tried to encourage him. The problem was Bernie's. I believe he despised himself. To say he loathed himself may sound harsh, so maybe it would be more acceptable if I referred to his insecurity, or his lack of self-worth.

Regardless of the term we use, Bernie didn't like himself very much. Had he liked himself, I'm convinced he would have been open to taking in new information. Because he didn't like himself, he wrapped protective arms around his ego and his writing projects. He never changed, and, of course, Bernie never published.

I can easily point out Bernie's flaws—he's somebody else— but we don't readily recognize our own. Whenever we close ourselves off from listening to others' suggestions, it speaks more about our self-attitude than it does about the speaker.

Maybe we're afraid of being shown that we're not efficient or bright or don't know what we're talking about. Perhaps it means we dislike ourselves so much we can't allow anything to shed light on our inner person. To admit we're less than what we'd like to be might cause us to fall apart.

One way of seeing this is that all of us have a view of ourselves that some have called the Ideal Self. That's who we'd like to be and actually think we are. It's not our Real Self. The more mature and open we are, the more the Real Self and the Ideal Self converge and we find inner harmony.

For example, on my first day of seminary, I chatted with Martin. Although we talked about a number of things, I specifically recall that he said, "I'm very good at languages, so Greek will be no problem to me."

At the end of the quarter, our mailboxes were near each other and I saw him take out his report card. He stared at his grades, his face drained of color, and he seemed frozen. "I failed," he mumbled.

I didn't see all his grades, but I did see that in the two courses in the biblical area, both of which required the use of Greek, he had received an F.

He turned brusquely and rushed out of the building. The next day I heard that he had withdrawn from seminary. His ideal—that he was excellent with languages—clashed with the reality that he wasn't.

Another way we despise ourselves is with our own words. My theory is that those we label as know-it-all types may be the weakest and most vulnerable. They have to prove they're right; to admit being wrong is a blow they can't handle. They're safer and far more secure if they don't listen or if they find excuses not to pay attention. ("Who do you think you are?" "Who elected you president of the company?") If they tell others quickly, and perhaps even a little loudly, it may shut up those voices, and then others won't probe any deeper. Naturally, the know-it-alls would come out ahead if they listened to good advice, but sometimes they're too inwardly frightened to do so. It's easier to shriek out the flaws of others than to search ourselves.

I learned years ago that what we despise in others may really be what we detest about ourselves. Here's an example of what I mean. During the years we lived in Kenya, East Africa, one co-worker upset me every time we met. One day I complained about him to Shirley. I particularly remember saying that he was loud-mouthed and self-opinionated and that he acted as if he knew everything.

Shirley listened quietly and nodded. Then she rubbed my cheek softly and kissed me. "Yes, I know, dear, and you're just like him."

Immediately, I wanted to defend myself, but Shirley had spoken so disarmingly, and I listened to what she said. I didn't like it or want to hear those words, but I also knew she was right.

That moment didn't produce any kind of instant healing, but it took me a long way on my journey. Through the years, that loving rebuke has reminded me how easily I can spot rigidity and lack of self-worth in others. Sometimes we who think we're listening and accepting instruction may be quietly rejecting it and seeing the flaws only in others.

When we see shortcomings in others, maybe their faces are really only reflecting what they perceive in us! Part of our maturing process is to accept the things we don't like about ourselves.

Modern Proverb: *We hurt ourselves when we reject instruction. It's smarter to listen carefully, even if it's not what we want to hear.*

Sacrifice or Prayer?

*The sacrifice of the wicked is an abomination to the
LORD, but the prayer of the upright is his delight.*
                                                    Proverbs 15:8

"Which is more important," the missionary asked, "to pray
faithfully for me in my work in Africa or to send me money
when it puts you in a financial bind?"

Although I was a college student when I heard that question, it forced me to think about two important things—praying and giving. In this case, the giving was money, but the
missionary meant more than that.

Most of us students had little money and barely scraped by.
For us to give any money would have been a hardship for us,
and he was wise enough to know that.

Until he asked, I had never thought about the difference
between praying and giving—or a better way to say it biblically—between prayer and sacrifice.

Modern readers have a difficult time with the idea of sacrifice because we've passed beyond those unenlightened cultures when people feared gods and did everything possible to
appease their wrath. They slaughtered animals as part of that
holy ritual. All through the Bible, the Jews presented their sacrifices to the priests. If they brought a lamb or a goat, the priest
offered it to God. For those who couldn't afford to offer animals, the Old Testament listed alternative offerings, all the way
down to a handful of meal or a small bird. The idea was to
make the sacrificial system affordable to everyone.

Their reasons for sacrifice varied as much our reasons for
prayer: to ask for something, to seek forgiveness, to give
thanks, or to petition on behalf of someone else.

As I thought about this verse, it can easily sound as if it's contrasting prayer and sacrifice—and, of course, prayer comes out ahead. Most of us wouldn't even question that.

But perhaps we should.

We don't think of going to priests and having them slaughter and burn animals. From our modern perspective, we probably translate *sacrifice* to mean that we give up or surrender something, such as giving up chocolate or Coke during the Lenten season. Or sacrifice can be an act that costs us time or demands work—but only that which is "above and beyond" our normal activities.

We then go on to say that sacrifice is surpassed by prayer. We have elevated prayer to the highest and the most spiritual human act.

But what if the writers didn't mean that kind of contrast? (I don't think they did.) Although the proverb is meant primarily as a contrast between the wicked and the righteous, it's easy also to see sacrifice and prayer as contrasted. Maybe—and I think this is the case—it's trying to say that the issue isn't prayer or giving—the value and effectiveness depend on the person rather than the act itself.

Earlier, I mentioned the missionary's question—his contrast between whether it was better to pray or to give sacrificially. What a powerful question it was for me that day. It's also one I've pondered many times.

When the missionary asked his question, most of us—and maybe this says where we were in our lives—opted for giving. "And especially when it involves a hardship," one student answered. He probably spoke for most of us.

"I wonder," the missionary said. "Think about it some more."

"I don't think there's a difference," a female student near the front said. "Isn't it more a matter of giving or doing what you can? Isn't it more of doing what you're able to do without trying to say which is better?"

The missionary agreed with her, and then he went on to say that he knew we were poor students and that he wasn't asking us for money. "I'd like to ask you to make a commitment to pray for me," he said. "To pray—every day—for our work." He paused, smiled, and added, "And for some of you, that kind of ongoing commitment is a sacrifice."

Looking back at that scene, I've had another thought.

My understanding insists that there is no difference in God's eyes between our giving and our praying. Both express commitment on the same level as reading our Bibles, sharing our faith, and serving people in need. That's the real point, I believe, of this proverb. There are those who offer what they have, and it's the right thing for them to do. There are those who pray because that's what they can do, and it's the right thing for them.

I want to take this a little further, however, and say that sacrifice, or any kind of action, has no merit in itself. It's only when linked with genuine commitment that our actions count. Animal sacrifices in the Old Testament meant nothing by themselves. The effectiveness depended on those who offered. This proverb makes it clear that if the ungodly offered animals, it was an abomination; if the godly offered, it delighted God.

I like to think of sacrifice as an expression of the inner person. Those who seek to live close to their Creator need ways to express that desire. Put another way, what goes on inside us shows up on the outside. Those who love God find ways to express it through service or through time alone with God.

In fact, if we love God, we *will* show it, because it has to come forth in some form. Pharisees and legalistic leaders of Jesus' day wouldn't agree with that. They seemed to put the emphasis on doing the right behavior, no matter what was going on inside. Yet the Bible makes it clear that our commitments start within. If we love God, it will manifest itself. And whatever that manifestation, it delights God.

Modern Proverb: *If we love God, our prayers and actions are acceptable. If we don't love God, nothing we do can please Yahweh.*

The Stoning of Martha May

Death and life are in the power of the tongue, and those who love it will eat its fruits.

Proverbs 18:21

Few short stories stay with me, but "The Stoning of Martha May" affected my life. At times I've violated the lessons I learned from reading it, but my troubled conscience still reminds me.

At least thirty years ago I read the story, printed inside an adult take-home Sunday school paper. It concerned a young woman who came to church and tried to break into the clique of single adults. She had a lower economic background but tried to join with the more affluent members of the Sunday school class she visited. The others didn't treat Martha May nicely, and they whispered about her behind her back. Whenever they saw her do anything that could be interpreted in a negative light, they made sure everyone heard. Eventually Martha May dropped out of the church.

Even then, they didn't leave her alone but continued to talk about her. They spread vicious rumors about her lifestyle, and no one attempted to befriend or help her.

At the end of the story, Martha May died. I don't recall if it was from a botched abortion or perhaps the result of a reckless motorcycle ride. What I remember is that the narrator of the story confessed that she and the others at church had stoned Martha May to death. For stones, they used words—hard, hurting, death-giving words. They told stories and passed on every bit of gossip they heard. None of them felt compassion or reached out to her.

Over the years since I read that story, I've seen a lot of stoning around the church. Of course, the church has no exclusive claims to such cruelty. But somehow we like to think that the people who sing hymns and pray are beyond that kind of behavior. But too often, it is in the church that we encounter the biggest boulders hurled on top of others.

For example, I was the pastor of a congregation where Ora Mae was the champion stoner. She never missed an opportunity to belittle, criticize, or speak unkindly of others. If she didn't know all the facts, she had the kind of imagination that supplied them. It seemed strange to me that people knew the kind of person she was but they still listened, and by passing on the boulders, they stoned a lot of people. I got badly hurt several times by some carefully aimed rocks from her practiced hands.

A few months before she died, I visited her in the hospital. As her pastor, I tried to be friendly and kind, although I had heard many of the mean-spirited things she had said about me and about my family as well.

After I had been there perhaps six minutes, she said, "Nobody likes me at church. Oh, they speak to me, but they don't like me. I try hard to be friends, but no one really likes me." Tears flowed down her cheeks as she talked.

We talked a few minutes and then I made an attempt to get her to face her stoning of others, but she cut me off. "I'm just a frank person."

Yes, she was that.

As I watched her that day, I realized that Ora Mae was reaping the fruit of her labors. It's the old principle of reaping what we sow, but it was the clearest illustration I've ever seen.

Within a month she returned to church, but she never changed. Until she died, she remained the most accurate stone-thrower I ever met. One deacon said, "At least she's democratic—she never overlooks anyone."

Not only did Ora Mae gather the fruit she had planted, but she operated on a sound principle we find in several places in Proverbs. The tongue—that is, the words we speak—is a powerful instrument. With that vocal instrument, we can do immense good or we can commit amazingly evil acts. "Death and life are in the power of the tongue." That's an extreme way of talking, but it points out how much we affect other people by the words that pass our lips. And those words aren't just sounds that pop out. They're expressions of powerful feelings deep within us. The tongue gives away what we really think.

The book of Proverbs focuses more on the tongue's ability to wound or hurt than it does on its healing or encouraging. Maybe it's because the latter is obvious and we don't realize how much our words affect those who listen. In fact, almost every one of Proverbs' thirty-one chapters has something to say about spoken words and the trouble they cause.

Several admonitions about speaking appear within the book. Here are three:

1. *Say little.* "When words are many, transgression is not lacking, but the prudent are restrained in speech" (10:19). That doesn't mean shutting up or becoming unnecessarily taciturn. But it does mean that the less we say about others, the better off we are. The tendency is that the more words we speak, the more we tend to speak carelessly.
2. *Think first, then speak.* The word translated *rash* or *hasty* appears often in Proverbs, as in a rash temper, judgments, decisions, and actions. Rash words may be the worst we speak. We may open our mouths with the best of intentions, but sometimes our feelings tell off on us and we say things better left unsaid.
3. *Listen more.* Too many of us work hard to be better speakers, and most of us probably need more help in being better listeners.

Our words are powerful—that's the worst and the best about them. A friend said, "Some of us need to register our tongue with the authorities as a deadly weapon."

Even though what we say may be true, it doesn't mean God wants us to speak. It's far too easy to cut a person to shreds by our tone as well as the actual words. Sometimes we're in such pain ourselves we blurt out wounding words. That doesn't excuse us, but it may help us to be a little kinder to ourselves.

As I've thought more of Ora Mae through the years, I don't think she was really any kinder to herself than she was to others. How could she have been? To me, she was an extremely sad, empty woman. Because she hurt so deeply inside, it blinded her to others' pain—especially the pain she caused by her cruel words. Through words, we can give unlimited encouragement or tear down the strongest resolve.

Yes, words are powerful when used wrongly. However, the right ones spoken at the appropriate time can bring about wonderful, exciting changes in the lives of others. For instance, one major reason I'm a writer today is because a man named Charlie Shedd, a much-published writer, saw my first piece of writing. He wrote me a letter, which I still have, and said, "You can do it. You can become an outstanding writer."

Charlie's words have been my encouragement through many discouraging days and dozens of rejections.

As I think of how much his words did for me, I wonder what it would be like if all of us monitored our verbal messages. What would happen if we focused on using the power of our words to heal, encourage, and change lives?

Maybe we'll never know until we try it!

Modern Proverb: *With our words, we can kill or we can heal. The choice is ours.*

Winning and Winning

He who mocks the poor shows contempt for their Maker;
whoever gloats over disaster will not go unpunished.
Proverbs 17:5, NIV

My fifty-six-year-old friend David Morgan played "Trivial Pursuit" with four relatives who were half his age. He easily won the game. David enjoyed his moment of success; the others felt devastated by his triumph.

That's the way games go. Every winner emerges in front of at least one loser. In business, in wars, or in most competitive relationships, the victors win and gloat. That's the mentality that has permeated our culture. Win! Win! Win!

One night I watched part of a film on TV about two rival football teams who were preparing to play the championship game of the season. "No one ever remembers who came in second," said the coach. "We're gonna be first—number one! And then people will remember us!"

The players rallied around his pep talk. I didn't have to watch the last ten minutes of the film to know that they won the crucial victory. The film would end on a triumphant note, with upbeat music and cheering crowds.

I'm not against winning, and I'm not opposed to competition. I love to win whenever I compete in any contest. Of course, none of us wins every contest, game, business deal, or argument. The tragedy comes when we sneer or belittle those we have bested.

Proverbs doesn't speak against winning—only against the excessive attitude of winning. It condemns the gloaters and the boasters. It's a way of saying that winning doesn't make us superior and the losers inferior. It means that in a single contest or game, one of us came out ahead of the other.

When we make winning anything more than that, we may have moved into forbidden territory. "He who mocks the poor shows contempt for their Maker; whoever gloats over disaster will not go unpunished." The key words are *mock* and *gloat.* This proverb is about an attitude.

It's as if we earn a million dollars annually and then sneer at those who struggle to make mortgage payments. Doesn't such an attitude imply (probably correctly) that we measure our self-worth by our achievements and possessions?

So if we win a game or earn more each month, does that make us special? Superior? Better? Obviously not.

Again an example from a film, this one about auto racing. The hero narrowly wins the race at the conclusion. What happened to his number-one opponent got me thinking. The man tried to pull around him with some clever maneuver that failed. The driver's vehicle went out of control, crashed into the fence, and destroyed the car. Just then, the hero grinned, raised his right arm, and yelled exuberantly as he made the final turn and won the race.

He grinned and cheered. Isn't that a way of gloating? It wasn't enough, then, to win and to triumph over his opponent, but my viewing of the film said that he relished the defeat and destruction of the other racing car.

"It didn't happen to me," the hero of the film implies by his actions. "I kept control of my car." I wonder if that's the kind of thing Proverbs warns against—gloating over the troubles and disasters of others?

We hear the winners speak all the time. "If you had only done it my way . . ." or "I invested and then got out at the right time, but you stupid people stayed in too long and lost everything." The illustrations—unfortunately—go on endlessly.

Living the life of inner harmony doesn't deny the victory. In a film or in life, I wouldn't have expected the race driver to stop his car and not finish. Wouldn't it have been a better message, though, if his face had expressed a little sadness? At least a twinge of sorrow that his opponent had been wiped out? What if the other driver had died? (It was a comedy, so we knew the opponent would survive.)

Let's take this idea to another level. The outwardly successful achievers speak clearly: "I made mine, you make yours." Their attitudes as well as their actions make it clear that they don't want others to ascend the success ladder behind them. They'd rather reach the top and destroy the ladder. They'll do whatever is necessary to prevent others from achieving or reaching their level. They want to sit alone at the top of the hill and sneer at those below.

For many people in business, it's not enough to make more money or to work at a prestigious company. They have to "bury the competition" (a phrase I've heard often). They're filled with glee when rivals put up out-of-business signs.

Yet Proverbs brings an element into this situation that most of us who are high-level achievers don't consider—and we don't need to have a million dollars for this to apply to us. The proverb says that we mock the poor. That includes the "less fortunates" and anyone below our financial or social stratum. In short, the losers. When we gloat over our superiority or seek to bury the competition, the sages say we show contempt *for God.*

What a strange statement, I thought at first reading. Is it really saying that if we despise and look down on those we have defeated or won over, we're mocking God? Is it possible that this verse speaks of our inner-connectedness (or lack of it)? That is, what if our attitudes and actions toward people actually reflect our disposition toward the Creator? Isn't it conceivable that no matter how spiritual we may appear at a place of worship, the real test results show up in our day-to-day behavior? We strive to be and to do our best—that's not the problem. The issue is how we treat those who don't win.

This proverb reminds me of an experience during my first year of seminary. The academic affairs committee set up a cash-prize contest among students to compete by writing about theological areas. I won first place in the biblical section and second in the theological.

A few days later, Alan, a third-year student who had won first place for his theological paper, saw me in the hallway. He rushed over and shook my hand. "I hope you don't mind, but I read your paper this morning. You did a masterful job."

I don't recall what I answered—something modest, I hope. "I wish we both could have won first place," he said.

When he said those words, I felt as if I had won the top prize—well, almost that good.

That memory has stayed with me through the years. I can't recall his last name, but I remember his generous spirit—the attitude that is so in line with this verse from Proverbs.

Alan had won, but winning was definitely not everything. His attitude, reflected by his behavior, said he was truly a winner because he made me feel like one. He could have despised me for being "only second." He chose the better way—to see me as an equal and to show me the respect of another winner.

We can turn the proverb around. Instead of looking at it negatively, we can look at it from a positive perspective. Instead of condemning the mockers, we can applaud the encouragers. We can focus on rewards and blessings instead of punishment.

And if we do, we probably will make God smile.

Modern Proverb: *Those who encourage others are the real winners. They are the ones who receive divine blessings.*

See How They Run

The wicked flee when no one pursues, but the righteous are as bold as a lion.

Proverbs 28:1

"Go on! Talk a little longer! Maybe your god had to go to the toilet, so keep on screaming. Try it again." Those weren't the exact words, but they were close to what the prophet Elijah meant.

What boldness! One man who stood alone in the midst of a threatening environment. In the presence of King Ahab, he challenged 450 prophets of the pagan god Baal to let their god prove himself. They built an altar on top of Mount Carmel and called on their god to burn up the animal offering without the priests lighting a fire. They cried, screamed, and yelled most of the day, but nothing happened.

Finally, the bold prophet had workers dig a trench around his sacrifice and liberally douse the animal and the stones with water. After Elijah prayed, a fire zipped down from heaven, burned the sacrifice, and lapped up the water. The entire story is found in 1 Kings 18, and it speaks of the kind of boldness even Elijah's enemies must have admired.

I share that story because it has helped me to understand this verse from Proverbs: "The wicked flee when no one pursues, but the righteous are as bold as a lion." For a long time I had wondered what meaning the sages wanted to convey. I'm convinced it's one of many sayings that contrast the righteous and the wicked. I'm just not sure that most of the people I know fit within their defined categories.

The most obvious thing is that the wicked run because of having a bad conscience. The statement may be a direct reference to Leviticus 26:17, where the context centers on the penalties for disobedience, especially the last statement: "I will set my face against you, and you shall be struck down by your enemies; your foes shall rule over you, and you shall flee though no one pursues you." Twice in Deuteronomy we get the same image of the guilty running from their enemies.

When we hit the second part of Proverbs 28:1—about the righteous being bold as a lion—it speaks of a fierceness in opposing the wicked. This part may be easier to grasp. It's a promise of divinely given courage to fight and win over our enemies. In the early verses of Leviticus 26, God promised they would triumph over their foes if their cause was just and if they obeyed.

The problem comes because we don't see much evidence of the wicked fleeing. In fact, we tend to see the reverse— Christians running and unbelievers standing boldly. But if we move beyond the mere words and think of the implication of the saying, it may help us understand what the sages wanted us to grasp.

First, let's consider the wicked. It's easy to speak of their bad consciences or the load of guilt—and I believe many carry heavy loads of shame and guilt. However, we live in a more sophisticated world, where we're able to hide those things a little better.

Today people still run, but they may not know why they're running. Augustine, one of the great thinkers of the fifth century, made the famous statement that we're restless until we find our rest in Jesus Christ. That's a form of running—just being restless, on the go, unable or unwilling to pause and reflect, to examine our lives, to ponder the things that really matter. In short, it's a picture of those who continually reject God. Carl Jung once said that people don't really solve the issues of life until they make their peace with God. That's flowing in the same direction as this proverb.

See how they run!

I see it all the time—people always running by buying, acquiring, or adding to what they already have. They keep looking for that elusive something that will make their lives content and worthwhile, or that will drive away their inner pain. They choose to run in the wrong direction.

I remember years ago reading about the death of the Oscar-winning actor George Sanders. He had had five marriages and a vast number of love affairs, and had been one of the most respected men in his profession, with a career that spanned thirty years. When he took his own life, he left a note that said, "Life is a bore."

I wonder if George Sanders had been fleeing and just got tired of running.

Second, let's examine the righteous. When we know we're living lives to honor God, that gives us courage. Maybe inner conviction is a better word. We can take a stand and nothing will move us.

That's not the same as being obstinate or stiff-necked—and we have plenty of those people around us. The kind of lionlike boldness that Proverbs extols comes from inner empowerment and often shows itself with calm firmness.

The most impressive story I know of this involved a British missionary and her ordeal after Belgium gave the Congo its independence. For years, there was murder, mayhem, cannibalism, rape, and every imaginable atrocity.

The one thing I remember most was that she told us a rebel soldier pressed a gun into her temple and smirked. "You say you believe in God? Are you ready to die?"

She understood exactly what he wanted. If she said, "Yes," she had no doubt that he would have pulled the trigger. If she answered, "No," he would have laughed at her faith.

"I stared right at him," she said. "All fear left me and I sensed God's loving presence. So I said, 'God knows.'"

That wasn't the answer the rebel wanted. Two more times he asked and she gave him the same answer.

He struck her across the face and walked away. She had spoken with the inner conviction that made her as bold as a lion.

That woman's kind of lionlike boldness comes from knowing that we are serving God. The godly boldness at its best is that calm, inner strength advocated by people like Rosa Parks, who refused to give up her seat on the bus because she was black. Other courageous men and women opposed racial laws because they were wrong. And knowing they were right empowered them. They didn't scream, insult, kick, or argue. *They didn't need to.* Like Elijah in his day, such people stood firm. Their just cause gave them the courage to face everything that came against them.

They've set the example. Now we know the way—if we're willing to follow it.

Modern Proverb: *God's people have a holy boldness that allows them to stand up against wrongdoing or evil. The wicked have no such inner strength.*

In Control

When the wicked die, their hope perishes, and the expectation of the godless comes to nothing.

Proverbs 11:7

Maybe it's part of being a human being, or maybe it's the defiance that comes from what theologians call our sinful nature. Whatever it is, we all like to live with the illusion that we're in control. We want to believe we have power over our feelings, lives, relationships, and especially our destinies. "I'm in charge here," we say. Too often we believe our words. Some of us go further and try to exert control over the lives and destinies of those around us. A few people believe they actually can have dominion over all the forces and situations around them.

I wonder if that wasn't part of the lure of eating the forbidden fruit in the Garden of Eden. If Adam and Eve ate, they would be in charge. They would make the choices about their lives, and because they would soon know good and evil, that would give them the ability to make wise choices.

We all know how wrong they were.

Although he spoke about worry and anxiety, Jesus also made it clear who's really in charge of the world and the circumstances around us: "Look at the birds of the air; they neither sow nor reap nor gather into barns, and yet your heavenly Father feeds them. Are you not of more value than they? And can any of you by worrying add a single hour to your span of life?" (Matthew 6:26–27).

Earlier I used the word *illusion*. Despite all that we can do to provide for every contingency in our lives, we still have to contend with factors that intrude unpredictably or that remain

48

outside our ability to control. We like to live with the self-delusion that we are the rulers of our lives.

My friend Stan began to invest online in the stock market in the 1990s. He studied the market well, watched growth trends, and took careful note of warning signs. By 1997, Stan had it all figured out and the money was coming in. He cornered me one day, paper and pen in hand, and showed me the shrewdness of his investments. He then declared, "By 2001, I can conservatively expect to be worth five million dollars."

Stan didn't take into consideration one significant factor: He wasn't in control of the stock market. The bullish market made some downturns and that reduced some of his anticipated earnings. On the whole, most of his stocks continued to do fairly well, but he had miscalculated on two investments. Both corporations are still alive—barely—but neither has earned money for the past two years. His investments, instead of being in the seven-figure range, barely reach $200,000. Don't get me wrong: I'm not writing against the stock market; rather I'm speaking against the kind of human arrogance that imagines it can control anything that happens to us.

I wonder what happened to Pharaoh's infallible plans to build more pyramids. How could he have foreseen that the slaves would revolt and drain the labor pool? Or what about Saul? God had elevated that farmer and made him king over Israel. One day, impatient because the priest Samuel had not arrived, he violated the commands of God. He, a non-priest, dared to offer a sacrifice, but then, he was the king. Because of that arrogant act, God told Samuel that he was to anoint David to succeed Saul.

Whether we're among the good or the evil, the principle still applies. And, yes, the good people too often forget who's really in control of their lives. It speaks of human arrogance when we declare what we're going to do and when we're going to do it, as if we have life all planned out.

I've been there all too often myself. For instance, during my first year of college, I had it all planned so that I'd have my doctoral degree within seven years and teach for the next forty. In my mind it was all worked out, because I hadn't allowed for divine intervention. In looking back over my life, I can say that God had much better plans for me. I hadn't counted on the many detours that life would offer me, and certainly I hadn't accounted for the roads that weren't listed on my map of life planning.

The sages point out two significant facts through this passage. First, they refer to the wicked—and today we'd say those who claim no relationship to God. Such people die, and when they do, it's all over for them. In days when the Old Testament was still being written, the concept of life after physical death wasn't known or fully understood.

Instead, they emphasized living to please God. Such an attitude would, they believed, result in surviving to a ripe old age with many descendants. At death, they passed on everything to their children and their children's children. That may be a bit difficult for people today to grasp because we don't think that way. But for them, the good life of God's favor and blessings continued on through those who bore their name.

When the wicked finished their physical existence, they stared into the face of death, and they had nothing left. All their planning, all their scheming, and all their control came to nothing. They were powerless to prolong their own lives.

What a shock some people today have. They strive to attain the best of everything, only to learn how empty their lives have been. They may have thought they had power, but ultimately, they were as helpless as every other human being who has crossed the dark river.

It doesn't take much digging to look at the sad end of some of those powerful magnates or power brokers. A generation ago, Howard Hughes amassed one of the greatest fortunes in the world, but he became a recluse, plagued with mental illness. Adolf Hitler had a grand scheme of controlling all of Europe, if not the world, but we know his end.

We don't have to point to the notorious or famous; we only have to look around us. So much of what we do in day-to-day decision making says, "This is my life. I can do with it as I choose."

Maybe?

No, not even maybe.

God is sovereign, and no matter how thoroughly any of us plan, we don't have the wisdom or the foresight to figure in all the conflicting factors and to control events or circumstances.

The book of James says this nicely. "You should know better than to say, 'Today or tomorrow we will go to the city. We will do business there for a year and make a lot of money!' What do you know about tomorrow? How can you be so sure about your life? It is nothing more than mist that appears for only a little while before it disappears. You should say, 'If the Lord lets us live, we will do these things.' Yet you are stupid enough to brag, and it is wrong to be so proud" (James 4:13–16, CEV).

Yes, it's pride at work when we try to control all the forces. James makes it clear that we plan, but if we're wise, in the midst of our planning, we'll add, "If the Lord lets us live." In times past, many Christians commonly added "God willing" in making their plans. Maybe it's something we need to think more seriously about.

To add "God willing" or a similar phase may sound awkward, and the words don't readily flow from our lips. Yet to make such statements is a powerful way to remind ourselves that we don't really have control. We can plan, hope, desire, and look forward to results. But the wise are those who say, "This will happen if it pleases God."

And, for those who follow God, it gives us assurance to read a divine promise: ". . . By his mighty power at work within us, he is able to accomplish infinitely more than we would ever dare to ask or hope for" (Ephesians 3:20, NLT).

God really has the best plans.

Modern Proverb: *The wicked may plan, but when they die, it's all over. If we obey God, our deeds live on forever.*

Being Good

The righteous are delivered from trouble, and the wicked get into it instead.

Proverbs 11:8

"Being good has its own reward," she said. "If we are good, God will bless us and we'll enjoy our life."

I was probably nine years old, and it was one of my few excursions into a worship service. Everyone called the woman preacher Sister Newcomb. I recall only that she had long white hair, which she braided and stretched around her head. Inside or outside the church, she never wore anything but white.

As she spoke, I thought her words sounded stupid. Many times, I had tried to be good; I found it boring as well as impossible behavior to maintain. With my limited exposure to Christianity, I thought there was nothing to it except following strict and often difficult rules. In fact, most of the rules told people what they couldn't do. *So why would that be a reward?* I wondered.

"Being good is good for you," she proclaimed. She seemed to be staring at me when she raised her voice and the words thundered out. She raised her right arm with its long, dangling sleeve, and her fingers seemed to point right at me. "Being bad is bad for you now and for eternity." For what must have been another twenty minutes she listed all the bad things that tripped up God's people, from alcohol to movies.

As I listened, I assumed that the second part was probably right—being bad was bad for us. In fact, I thought at the time, I knew that already. When I did something wrong, I usually got found out, and then I got spanked or scolded.

Now that I'm older, I've looked at this matter of being good or bad in a different light. To my surprise, I have to admit that goodness *does* carry its own reward. I've learned, for instance, that when I've done the right thing at the right time, I've experienced peace. I've had the inner assurance that my life is going to get better, and sometimes my being good has also helped to improve life for others.

This proverb goes on to say that if we're good—which means that we're living in obedience to God—we're delivered from trouble. One translation puts it this way: "God rescues the godly from danger" (NLT). By serving God, we can rightly expect some reward for our commitment. Aside from answered prayer and assurance of salvation, doesn't the relationship also include God guiding us so we don't walk onto the thin ice of the frozen ponds?

Isn't rescuing and shielding from danger part of the work of the Holy Spirit in our lives? I sincerely believe so. And as I've thought about this, I can think of two ways in which God provides escape from our troubles.

First, if we're sensitive to God, we receive warnings in a variety of forms. We can name them premonition, intuition, or "just a feeling," or we can give it a biblical tag, by referring to "the utterance of knowledge" (1 Corinthians 12:8). Some people are more sensitive in picking up on the subtle warnings than others. One woman told me, "I just get a-knowing inside."

Many of us, afraid of being thought of as strange when we speak or respond from the feeling level, hesitate to share experiences of those divine interventions in our lives. Yet I'm convinced that such experiences are available for God's people, and they're the means by which God makes us aware of impending pitfalls. I like to think of it as living by faith—that is, we open ourselves to guidance that comes to us apart from facts and hard evidence. For me, it's knowing without knowing how we know.

Here's an example of that knowing-without-knowing in my life. In late September, a woman contacted me to help her write her autobiography. I'd been a professional ghostwriter for fourteen years and had made a good living at it. I wanted to move into doing more books of my own (such as this one) and had turned down seven or eight people who had approached me in the previous year.

When the woman phoned, within ten minutes, she convinced me. Her story sounded exciting and significant. A few days later I received newspaper and magazine articles about her. Everything said, "This is a can't-lose project." I talked to my agent, and based on my take of the story, she readily agreed.

Over the next two months, the woman and I had additional correspondence, e-mails, and several phone calls. The more she contacted me and talked to me, the more something didn't feel right. I didn't want to speak up, or maybe I wasn't ready to say, "This growing reservation is God speaking." Despite those tiny warning bells in the background, all the outward evidence kept shouting, "This is a powerful story."

One November night I couldn't sleep. After maybe three hours, I realized that the project troubled me. I asked God to help me know what to do. The more I prayed, the more clearly I felt that I didn't want to work with the woman.

Here's where the problem came in for me. If I declined—after nearly two months of talking and discussing—what should I tell her? After all these weeks, how could I explain that it just "didn't feel right"?

I didn't know why it wasn't right, and I couldn't point to anything specifically—just that inner discomfort. So I tried to talk myself out of such feelings.

Still no sleep. Finally, at 2:30 in the morning, I knew I couldn't do her book. I got out of bed and wrote her a letter. "God, please let me go to sleep now. If this is right for me to send, let me go to sleep, and make me feel the same way tomorrow." I went to sleep almost immediately.

The next morning, I felt even more certain I needed to decline.

In the letter I wrote, I simply said, "I can't do it." I avoided giving a reason, because I didn't want to get into defending my decision.

The woman phoned, but I held to my position, although I did start citing reasons, such as already having a busy schedule (true) and needing to have a little more free time (also true). Then she called my agent and complained about me (she got nowhere). The woman wanted to come and see me "so we can get this thing straightened out." I said no and remained firm.

She e-mailed me. She mailed me more material. At least once a week she phoned.

It took almost two months before she left me alone. The last I heard of her, she was driving another writer half-crazy with phone calls. I was truly thankful to be out of the situation.

Now, long past that experience, I've reviewed the situation. Was that really God nudging me to get out of the deal? Was that the Holy Spirit preventing me from sleeping and causing me to have a troubled night? Yes. I have no doubts.

As a believer, I find it fairly easy to say, "God delivered me from trouble." I can't, however, say I've always listened to that voice or accepted God's help, but I'm learning. The deliverances may not always be powerful or dramatic, but they are real.

Second, God delivers us once the trouble has struck. Never in the Bible do we find a promise that we won't suffer the same problems, hardships, and difficulties that happen to everyone else. The difference is that we have a spiritual resource in the midst of our troubles. We have a loving, compassionate, ever-watchful God, who is there to save us—often from our own folly.

As we learn to hear God's quiet speaking, the divine whisper, the slight nudge of the Spirit, we cope better and trouble no longer overwhelms us. We learn to put up barriers to the problems.

God doesn't usually whisk us out of the midst of troubles. In fact, part of the reason we need God is so that we can go through the trials of life. "No testing has overtaken you that is not common to everyone. God is faithful, and he will not let you be tested beyond your strength, but with the testing he will also provide the way out so that you may be able to endure it" (1 Corinthians 10:13).

God performs miracles when we need them—those moments

of perfect timing, the right word spoken by a friend, a phone call from an unexpected source when we're asking God what to do next. Most of us have experienced those moments when the guidance of God is clear or the seemingly impossible turns into reality.

Here's how I look at it. God, our Loving Parent, delivers us by letting us go through minor crises so that we won't repeat them and fall into major ones. The more closely we listen to God speaking, the more we find deliverance before we fall into pitfalls and problems.

Modern Proverb: *The people of God find deliverance when trouble comes. Others don't have such spiritual resources.*

Confessing Sins

*No one who conceals transgressions will prosper, but
one who confesses and forsakes them will obtain mercy.*
Proverbs 28:13

God and humans both cover sin. God does so by grace;
humans do it through shame and hypocrisy.

This proverb points out that hiding our sins or denying our
failures doesn't work. We get found out. If we turn to God, this
proverb says, we obtain mercy. In other places in the Old
Testament, the writers call it forgiveness.

As I thought about hiding our sinful actions, immediately I
remembered the story of Adam and Eve in the garden. With all
the bountiful provisions of God, they received only one negative command: Do not eat of the tree of the knowledge of good
and evil.

When they disobeyed that command and ate, the Bible says,
"Then the eyes of both were opened, and they knew that they
were naked; and they sewed fig leaves together and made loin-
cloths for themselves" (Genesis 3:7).

That was history's first human cover-up. It had nothing to
do with their bodies, but with an awareness that they had done
wrong. They experienced something called shame—a feeling
of wrongdoing and a knowledge of unworthiness. They did the
most natural thing—a practice we still follow—they tried to
hide it, to push it away, and to act as if it hadn't happened.

In the millennia since, we haven't changed much in our
behavior. Maybe part of being imperfect and sinful is that we
automatically want to conceal our wrongdoing. Maybe it's
because we want others to see only the good things about us,
to respect us and admire our honorable qualities. So we try to

57

hide the truth. It's as if we think that if we dig a hole deep enough and bury our wrong behavior, we won't know it still exists and no one else will find out.

We delude ourselves. We don't forget; the wrongdoing stays within us, and we add to the load we carry through other failings. Without confessing, we're eventually worn out with carrying a heavy weight.

John Bunyan illustrated this in his delightful allegory, *The Pilgrim's Progress*. Christian carries a heavy load on his back that weighs him down. When he finally sees the cross, the heavy load rolls away. That's our initial forgiveness by God.

Too many of us have been to the cross—and that may be our problem. That is, we had an initial experience with Jesus Christ and committed ourselves to follow the Savior. Then what happens the next time we fail? And there will always be a next time and a time after that and still times after that.

We can deny our failures or we can hide the actions from ourselves and from others. Or we can take the courageous path and confess. Along with confession comes forsaking, according to this proverb.

One way to see how this works is to look at the Old Testament view of restitution. Beyond acknowledging and leaving our sin, we also need to make things right. For example, in the Old Testament, thieves had to repay four times what they had stolen. In the story of Jesus and Zacchaeus, the tax collector met Jesus and invited the teacher into his house. Afterward, Zacchaeus came out and announced, "'Look, half of my possessions, Lord, I will give to the poor; and if I have defrauded anyone anything, I will pay back four times as much.' Then Jesus said to him, 'Today salvation has come to this house . . .'" (Luke 19:8–9).

As we consider the matter of sin and confession, the Bible stresses *our* need to confess. After all, God knows what we've done. If we try to hide or cover up, as Adam and Eve tried to do, we only fool ourselves.

I think the Garden of Eden story is a laughably sad tale. After they sinned, the Bible says God walked into the garden and saw them and they were different. They had covered their bodies. Could they have been so foolish to believe God wouldn't have noticed they were different? This says that we can't cover up successfully.

This proverb makes clear the choices we face. If we confess, we experience mercy—that means *divine forgiveness.* Not to confess is the voice of pride that says, "I don't need confession," or "I can handle this myself." True, some simply don't perceive the extent of divine forgiveness and say, "My sin is too great," even though the Bible emphatically points out that God lovingly forgives all our sins.

Another factor we need to think about is what confession does for *us.* When we first come to a relationship with Jesus Christ, we're assured that we're forgiven. We're told that Jesus died for *all* our sins. That's true, and it includes those we have not yet committed.

So why confess? Simple. *We* need cleansing and know it. We need to take off the fig leaves and open up our nakedness once again to God. To do so makes us accountable. It also enables us to see more of God's love and compassion. When we confess, it's saying, "God, you have given us laws and I have broken them."

"Yes, and you are forgiven," God whispers. "Now go and sin no more."

Confession also does something else for us—it makes us change our ways. Zacchaeus, a tax collector, a collaborator with Rome, bought his job and made profit by defrauding people and collecting more money than he paid Rome. We have no idea what went on while he ate with Jesus, but we do know the results—he was transformed. He promised to put things right.

Confession, then, isn't to produce shame or to make us feel guilty. Perhaps it helps if we think of confession and the resulting shame or guilt as divine methods to attain specific goals. Jesus once said to the Pharisees that those who are well don't need a doctor. He meant that only as we're aware of our sickness, our burdens, our unconfessed sins, do we take any kind of action.

Implicit in the act of confession is the promise to change. Then we get to the purpose behind it all. God wants us to grow and to change.

To put it biblically, God has a specific purpose for us, and yet I rarely hear people acknowledge this purpose: It is to grow so that we increasingly become more like Jesus Christ, the Perfect One. Here's an oft-quoted, but easily overlooked, statement of that fact: "We know that all things work together for good for those who love God, who are called according to his purpose . . . to be conformed to the image of his Son, in order that he might be the firstborn within a large family" (Romans 8:28–29).

It's really that simple. God loves us enough to demand the best of our lives. When we detour onto the crooked path, our consciences trouble us until we confess. By that simple act of obedience, we get off the crooked path, and we're a lot more careful and faithful about following the straight path.

Modern Proverb: *If we confess our failures, God forgives us, and we learn to like ourselves a lot more.*

PART TWO

Living with the Family

To Spank or Not to Spank

He who spares the rod hates his son, but he who loves him is careful to discipline him.

Proverbs 13:24, NIV

They knocked on our door late one afternoon and introduced themselves as friends of our friends. They needed a place to spend the night. We lived in an isolated part of East Africa, and we welcomed the company.

By the end of the introductions, I knew we faced a serious problem. The problem's name was Tommy—the couple's son, who was maybe three years old. The difficulty started while we still stood on our cement porch. The boy saw flowers in our yard, scampered down the three steps, and headed toward them.

We lived in a dry area with poor soil and high altitude. Friends from the wet, sea-level, coastal area had given us eight tiny indigenous plants that weren't suited for our climate or high altitude. It had taken a lot of effort for me to make the plants live. The three-month-long dry season when we got absolutely no rain was nearly over. Out of eight plants, three had survived the relentless heat and lack of moisture.

The boy snatched the bloom off one plant.

"Tommy, don't do that," Dad said. "The man won't like it."

Mom, who had been talking to my wife, hadn't noticed and didn't look around.

Tommy, busily examining the flower in his hand, said nothing. I watched his fingers trace the softness of the off-white bloom. He held it to his nose and inhaled the sweet odor. Dad stood next to me and went back to his conversation about the long drive that way.

The boy pulled the bloom off the second plant and Dad said, "Now don't do that, Tommy. The man won't like it." The child reached for a third flower.

I jumped off the porch, raced forward, grabbed the boy by the shoulders, and carried him to the porch. "Don't do that, Tommy. This man doesn't like it."

The parents made no comment on what I had done.

Until they left the next morning, I had to keep Tommy in my line of vision. If I was around, he behaved. If I left the room or was out of eyesight, he'd start misbehaving. One time, I walked back into the room and he was pulling the stuffing out of one of Shirley's hand-sewn pillows.

I held up an index finger. Tommy stared for a moment and then dropped the pillow. Mom didn't notice his actions, and Dad, in the middle of a story, paid no attention.

Dad and Mom never disciplined the boy. Occasionally, they yelled at him to stop, but they never followed through or did anything to stop him.

What should they have done?

When I told a friend about the experience, he said, "Yeah, spare the rod and spoil the child." He wasn't quoting Proverbs 13:24 accurately, but he voiced the attitude of many.

For centuries this proverb has provided ample reason to spank, whip, or beat. Today the spanking or not spanking has become an attitude of serious debate. Many defend the practice and point to their own lives. "If I ever tried to sass my dad, I got my bottom blistered," said one of my friends. They quickly support that with further quotes from Proverbs, such as 29:15: "The rod of correction imparts wisdom, but a child left to itself disgraces his mother" (NIV).

Others, of course, oppose the idea and say, "No spanking! It's violence, and such behavior provokes and teaches violence."

I don't know either way about spanking. I suppose it finally comes down to personal understanding, temperament, and maybe even cultural mores. However, I do know the *principle* involved. And that principle isn't really about whether to spank.

The Bible comes to us in the language of the ancient culture of Israel. A beating—and often a harsh one—was the price children paid for not doing exactly what they were told. In other primitive cultures, parents could have their children put to death for disobedience.

Proverbs 13:24 isn't about corporal punishment. The principle is stated first negatively and then positively: "He who spares the rod hates his son, but he who loves him is careful to discipline him" (NIV).

Negatively, it says that if we don't discipline, this shows that we hate our children. Rather harsh words to state that to refrain from punishing equals hatred of the child. Taking this into our modern culture, here's where I think the proverb wants us to go: If parents love their kids, they set them straight. If they don't love them, they let the children get away with bad behavior.

Maybe that's truer than most of us want to admit. Is it possible that the more we love them, the more we try to enable them to live among other people and outside our walls? Could it be that indifference and overlooking their misbehavior means that we—their parents—don't really care?

Here's the way I would rewrite the proverb for us today: "If you don't care about your kids, you'll let them get away with anything. If you love them, you'll discipline them."

And all children need discipline. Our children showed us the complexity of this situation. Our oldest, Wanda, usually needed only to hear the anger in my voice. At most, one slap on her bottom was enough. (That was before anyone questioned spanking.) Our third child, John Mark, was one of those delightful, compliant children who heard us say no and obeyed without question.

By contrast, our middle child, C-C—much like her father—would never have yielded to corporal punishment. Once, when she was about five years old, I said to her, "If I spanked you until you died, you know what would happen? With your dying breath, you'd grit your teeth and moan *no.*"

C-C laughed because she knew it was true. However, she did respond when I put her on my lap, hugged her, and told her she had done wrong.

I believe that even though I treated all three of our children differently, I still followed the wisdom of those words.

I caught this clearly when I was working on a book about the family of Ruth and Fred Harris. That couple raised nine children, who have all lived exemplary and godly lives. One of the things Ruth said to me was "Oh, I spanked my children. I sure did. But I'll tell you something else I did. Before I spanked them, I made sure they knew why they were getting spanked. And when I finished, I hugged them and told them I loved them."

Here's why Ruth's words impressed me: She disciplined all nine of her children, but not in angry outbursts or frustration. When she spanked them, she made sure they knew they were loved.

Isn't that the point of the proverb?

Modern Proverb: *Those who love their children lovingly correct them; those who don't love their children allow them to go undisciplined.*

Training Programs

*Train children in the right way, and when old, they will
not stray.*

Proverbs 22:6

I can't think of a verse that parents quote more often during
children's rearing years, or groan about more after the children
are grown. This verse, intended to encourage, has been used
too often to induce guilt for those whose children haven't
turned out "right."

First, let's look at a few words. *To train* troubles translators.
Generally the Hebrew word refers to the beginning or start of
something, but it has other meanings. The sages urged, "Start
your children walking down the right path." In reading this
verse, I noticed that those wise thinkers refrained from laying
out any teaching method or describing content of that training.
"Start teaching them" is the exhortation.

Another meaning of the word is *to dedicate,* and it's used
that way only twice in the Old Testament. The first time it
refers to dedicating a house (Deuteronomy 20:5) and the second to Solomon's temple (1 Kings 8:63). The verb is *hanakh,*
and its noun form is the name of the Jewish feast of Hanukkah
that celebrated the rededication of the Temple in Jerusalem
under the Maccabees (165 B.C.).

In short, this proverb is saying, "Start the children out by
dedicating them to God. As you yourselves follow God and
lead them in the right way, they'll follow. After they're grown,
their lives will reflect that beginning."

But how and what do parents teach their children? Proverbs
implies that parents know the teachings of the Old Testament
and should begin to instruct their offspring by obeying the

teaching they themselves follow. Whatever parents see as those first steps, that's where they're to begin.

It seems evident that the training should begin as soon as possible. I remember reading an old textbook on education. Apparently a mother asked her pastor, "When should I begin to teach my child about God?"

"How old is your child?"

"He's seven."

"Hurry home, madam. You have already wasted the seven best years of your son's life. Don't waste any more."

True story or not, the point is valid. We can't begin too soon. We teach learning patterns before infants are aware of them. For example, fifty years ago, few churches provided nurseries. If they did, they didn't have any staff or helpers. Parents brought their infants with them and put them in bassinets on the pew or in the aisle. If the infants cried, the parents took them out, soothed them, and brought them back in.

I'm not trying to undo history, nor do I condone getting rid of nurseries. Those parents were training those infants, even those only weeks old, about how to behave in public. As the children grew older, they learned the music and the behavior simply by observing what went on around them in the services. Long before they can articulate it, children absorb the message they witness.

Whatever we teach children stays with them long after they're grown. That lays the burden on parents to decide what to teach and when. It also puts the burden on parents to realize that much of what the children learn from them isn't just what they intended.

This came across clearly to me during the first year I was a pastor. A couple came to me after they had been married two years and had no children. "A woman's place is in the home, and she needs to work there by doing the things a wife is supposed to do," the man insisted.

She pointed out that she had a better job than he did and brought in more money. He also admitted that he had a bad temper and rarely kept a job more than a year.

In our discussions, I finally asked why he insisted her place was in the home. If he had said, "I think that's a biblical principle," I figured we would have a good discussion point. "Because my father and mother lived that way. He never let her work."

I thought of those words, "He never let her work." His parents had taught him well—but I wondered if that was the message they wanted him to learn. (He remained so adamant in his position on that and other aspects of a wife's duties that eventually they divorced.)

That incident helped force me to realize how much we accept and believe as the "right thing" simply because that's how it was modeled at home.

The idea intended by this proverb is that if parents mold their children's behavior properly, they won't deviate from that way for the rest of their lives. Like many other proverbs, however, this is a general principle that's true in the vast number of cases. The trouble comes when we try to push it as an absolute rule. Or worse, when we take it as a promise.

As a kid, I remember a neighbor named Roy who beat his kids—not just spanking, but what we'd label as physical abuse today. One time when I was playing nearby, the police came because someone objected to all the noise.

Roy, who looked as if he had posed for a Mr. Universe contest, apologized to the police for the screaming of his children. "But I am exercising my God-given rights as a parent. God has promised me that if I raise these kids right, they won't depart from it." It was obvious to me, even as a kid of ten, that Roy was certain he was teaching them the right things. I doubt that he was. (They moved away so I don't know what happened.)

After my own conversion and after I had begun to read the Bible, I reflected quite a lot on that incident. I think Roy pulled that verse out of the Bible and latched onto it as a *promise* instead of a *principle*. That way, perhaps unconsciously, he could brutalize his children and, when challenged, justify his harsh behavior.

Most of those people don't get away with such harsh treatment of children today. Even so, there are still those who interpret this as an absolute, infallible promise. What they don't grasp is that these words—and most of the words of wisdom—are observations and general principles.

If we accept it as a principle, then the proverb lays an even stronger responsibility on the shoulders of parents to learn the best ways to train their children. No parents ever accomplish it perfectly, but it can lead them to being more careful, sensitive, and open to hearing God's directions.

Modern Proverb: *Start your children right by dedicating them to God. Then continue to teach them godly ways. If you do, they'll reflect the teachings they learned at home.*

Kids' Duties

A wise child loves discipline, but a scoffer does not listen to rebuke.

Proverbs 13:1

Listen to your father who begot you, and do not despise your mother when she is old.

Proverbs 23:22

Throughout the Bible, the one message for children is to honor their parents, which is the Fifth of the Ten Commandments. The New Testament commands children to obey their parents "for this is right" (Ephesians 6:1). The next verse begins, "Honor your father and mother," and links it with the Fifth Commandment by saying, "This is the first commandment with a promise"—which is well-being and long physical life.

To honor means to respect, but in today's culture, we don't always get the impact of this command. In ancient times, it wasn't unusual to live in the same house or immediately next to parents and even grandparents. Sometimes three or four generations lived together. As long as parents were alive, they received respect, honor, and obedience—even if the child was fifty years old! Among other things, respect meant caring for parents in old age—to care for them as they had cared for their young.

Several times in Proverbs we read verses that speak of the attitude toward fathers in one line and that toward mothers in the next. They used that as a poetic device. As pointed out earlier, the form, called the *mashal,* consists of two parallel lines in the Hebrew text, and the second line is *synonymous* with the first—that is, the second repeats the same idea in different words. It intends to include both parents, and it connects them with such words as *respect* and *honor.* Today, many of us have still-living parents even though we're parents ourselves. As we well know, having our own family doesn't absolve us from the responsibilities attached to us as children.

71

Proverbs lists several distinct responsibilities for those of us who are children to still-living parents.

God expects children of all ages to listen to their parents. (See also Proverbs 15:5; 23:22; 30:17.) When we're adults, it's much harder to obey than when we were nine years old. To listen doesn't mean that we have to follow everything they say, but it does mean to hear—that is, to understand—what they're saying. It's easy to close our minds and to think we know more because we live in a different world or we're better educated.

I think one way children learn to listen is to be listened to. Those children whose parents were patient and willing to hear the pains and troubles of the young get paid back in their old age—they get listened to.

Some of those kids who grow up showing contempt for their parents just may be the very people who saw that form of behavior modeled in their childhood. If their own parents didn't honor their parents, what kind of message did they learn?

Old Testament law legislated the response to rebellious and disobedient children who stubbornly refused to listen and learn at home. The worst pronouncement occurs in Deuteronomy 21:18–21, which commands stoning those children to death—this sounds totally abhorrent to us today. The idea wasn't based on an inflated idea of the vast wisdom of parents and that children had to obey. Rather, the command grew from the sense of the importance of the family unit. *This family unit, established by God, is the basis for all healthy human relationships.*

The family nourishes those within its bounds and prepares them to live in the community. Now, no children ever turn out to fulfill the perfect dreams of their parents. If they did, they probably would be some kind of robot, afraid to think for themselves.

The idea behind the law was that the family became nurturers and teachers. They prepared the young to live responsibly and harmoniously in their environment. By family instruction— formal and informal—they passed down covenant faith from generation to generation. (See Deuteronomy 6:4–7, 20–24.)

If children rebelled against the teachings of their parents, it was more than disobeying two individuals. They disobeyed

God's representatives and, hence, had turned against God! They were casting aside the divine institution for order and responsibility in society. I doubt that the Israelites stoned many children, but the law was there—possibly intended as a strong deterrent. I hope that, more than fearing the consequences of the law, they grasped the principle of the family unit. Faithful parents, dreading such a grave thing, would have worked diligently to keep their children living faithfully.

One of the most awful verses in the Bible about punishment occurs in Proverbs 30:17, and it's along the lines of an "eye for an eye." It reads: "The eye that mocks a father and scorns to obey a mother will be pecked out by the ravens of the valley and eaten by the vultures." In short, scoffing children face violent deaths. The idea is that such incorrigible children would be left as carrion for the birds. I assume that means they would first have been stoned and then left there. Ravens and vultures don't gouge out the eyes or devour human eyeballs unless the eyeballs are motionless—that is, unless the person is already dead. This ghastly image is displayed in the death of King Saul's sons. For a full week, Rizpah sat beside their bodies and chased away the vultures (2 Samuel 21:1–8).

As repugnant as that sounds, this violent threat was intended as the ultimate consequence for children's refusal to accept discipline and obey their parents.

Rather than a threat, I wonder if this isn't held up as a warning. Instead of using the idea to make children quake, maybe it's a way to say to parents, "If you faithfully honor God, by your example, you show your kids how to do it. You show by your faithful example." Is it just possible that this is more an admonition for the parents than for the children?

Modern Proverb: Children, honor your parents. When you do, you're honoring God. Parents, teach your children. When you do, you're honoring God.

Cursing Our Parents

*If you curse father or mother, your lamp will go out in
utter darkness.*

Proverbs 20:20

"Oh you can't talk about God as *Father* when you teach," a
Christian educator said quite pointedly at a teacher-training
conference. "It is one term we do not use." Around the room, I
saw nods and smiles.

No one challenged her. Finally, I spoke up. "Really? The
Bible contains many such references, in both Testaments, and
it was a wonderful way to explain God to the human race."

"Yes, but we live in a more enlightened age." She gave me
an indulgent smile as if I were in fifth grade. "You see, many
children today have had abusive and harsh parents. If we compare God to human parents—especially to our fathers—think
of what that implies. Many of those children have never known
a good father. Consequently, the meaning of Heavenly Father
will be useless."

"You think abuse was invented within the past decade?" I
asked. "They had the same problems in biblical times, I'm
sure, and—"

"Of course, they did, but we live in more enlightened times
and—"

"Besides, my father was an alcoholic and physically abusive," I said and raised my voice to equal hers. "Not once in
my life do I recall his being warm or tender. I can also tell you
something else. One of the major factors that drew me to the
Christian faith was that God represented the kind of father I
never had. God the Father filled a gap in my life, a need that
would never have been satisfied by my human father."

She refused to discuss what I said, restated her position, and moved on. That incident happened more than a decade ago. Yet I remain convinced more than ever that although individuals dishonor and demean their roles as mothers and fathers, we don't help children or anyone else by refusing to use terms such as the paternal or maternal side of God when we want to talk about human relationships.

We're born with an innate need to connect with our parents, to love and be loved by them, and if we don't receive it from them, we continue to search for that need to be met. Anyone who has worked with abused children can affirm that even after children have been repeatedly beaten by a mother or sexually assaulted by a father, they still cry out for that love they haven't received. They'll excuse the abuser, reach out to be hugged, and even insist on living with such adults.

I saw a film recently in which one of the major characters is a man who detests his father. The young man is now in his mid-thirties. When he was a teen and his mother was dying of cancer, his father deserted them. Later, the man gets notified that his dad is dying and wants to see him. He immediately reacts with outrage. "Where was he when I needed *him*?"

Another twenty minutes into the film, the son shows up at the father's bedside. He screams at the old man and curses him for all his rotten behavior and for deserting his family when they needed him most. Then the camera focuses on the son's face—tears fill his eyes and his voice cracks. Even while he's screaming out, he grabs his dad and hugs him.

That film depicted life accurately. We want—we need—to love and be loved by those who brought us into the world. Not only did God create us like that, but it's also part of being human. And that need *is* innate—not based on the behavior or conduct of the parents.

I emphasize that fact even though life doesn't always work out with happy talk and loving embraces. And it isn't new to our culture—the family conflict has always been around.

Today we tend to look at people individually and, thus, we respect those we like, or we honor those who have earned our respect. This runs contrary to the Old Testament and other ancient cultures. They considered the position or office more than the person. Parents, for instance, received *respect as parents* even if they failed to live up to societal expectations. The same attitude prevails in the New Testament, as in Ephesians 6:1–9 and 1 Peter 2:13–28.

Another way to say it is that if parents fail in their responsibilities, rather than expose them to reviling, cursing, or showing disrespect, children need to cover their shame. That is, they still respect them for being their parents, and love them simply because they are their parents.

This proverb reminds us of the Fifth Commandment—that those who honor their parents will live long on the earth. However, taking the downside, it warns that those who curse their parents will have their lamps snuffed out—that is, die young.

When the proverb says, "Your lamp will go out in utter darkness," it poetically refers to death, but it contains more than a warning. It holds the additional implication that the cursing ones will die without leaving behind their own families. For anyone to die childless was considered the worst shame and implied the displeasure of God.

Although this proverb doesn't say it, the proper response is to bless our parents—that is, to speak well of them, to honor them *simply because they are our parents.* Even if we feel our parents have failed, we can still be grateful for the good things they have done for us.

No parents are ever perfect, but like civil authorities or rulers, we respect the "office" they hold. The Bible also makes a case that those in such positions must one day give an account of themselves to God.

This verse emphasizes again that despite specific abuses, God ordained the family structure—a mother, a father, and children. Each has responsibilities to God. If the parents fail, this does not excuse the children for failing.

That's where the problem comes in. If we put this on a case-by-case basis, we can justify the cursing and despising. But if we put this on the level where the Bible puts it—as a principle—we'll respect the divinely appointed family unit and, even more, honor the God who set it all up.

Modern Proverb: *When we curse or speak evil of our parents, we speak evil of the divinely ordained human institution—the family—and God won't hold us guiltless.*

Gray Is Beautiful

The glory of youths is their strength, but the beauty of the aged is their gray hair.

Proverbs 20:29

Pat had just turned thirty-one when he went to Africa as a missionary. He's fair-skinned and has always looked younger than his actual age, even today when he's in his sixties. When he had his first meeting with African elders, he was with two other missionaries, both in their late thirties, and both with flecks of gray in their hair.

In the discussions, Pat stood up to make a point. "Sit down, *mtoto* (child)," one of the African elders said to him. "We will listen to the gray hairs first."

Pat realized an important fact—they respected age. He was older than some of those who called him a child, but they saw only what he looked like and didn't believe he could possibly have the wisdom of the older ones.

That respect for age is something we often overlook in our culture today. Not long ago, a woman in her late fifties said to me, "When a woman reaches a certain age in this country, she becomes invisible. She's no longer important."

She may have exaggerated the situation, but I think she expressed what many seniors feel—undervalued and unappreciated—as if those who are younger don't believe that from their years on this earth they've learned anything worth listening to. It hasn't always been that way, and in some cultures, age still brings respect.

This proverb says, "The glory of youths is their strength," and speaks of not only their physical stamina, but the power and capacity to enjoy those lives. Older people may lack vitality and often complain of their weakness, but they compensate for it by an accumulated lifetime of experience and wisdom.

Someone said to me, "The young represent physical strength; the old represent survival." He went on to say that it's a definite plus when they've acquired maturity through the process. They have learned much and can easily help those who are searching for guidance.

Here's a biblical example that shows the wisdom of the aged contrasted with the energy of the young. After King Solomon's death, his son and successor, Rehoboam, asked his father's advisers—all older men—for their advice about taxation. They urged him to lighten the load. Then he asked his young friends and they said, "Get tougher." He listened to the young men's foolish advice, and it resulted in the split-up of the nation. Ten of the twelve tribes pulled away and formed the Northern Kingdom of Israel.

Every stage of life has honor and privilege, of course, but the sages make a sharp contrast here. When the physical abilities diminish, the learned wisdom prevails—at least in the ideal. It takes a certain amount of living on this earth and going through hardships and failures for us to learn and live better.

I thought about the strength of the aged when my older brother died of cancer—on the day of my father's funeral. My siblings stood around, afraid to tell our then seventy-nine-year-old mother. "She's already so broken-hearted, this will kill her," one of them said.

In a moment of insight, I said, "Wait a minute. How do you think she's lived to be this old? She's tough—probably tougher than the rest of us. She's experienced loss and defeat and heartache. Of course it will hurt, but she'll handle it."

"Then you tell her," a sister said.

I did—and it was difficult—but Mom handled it well. Tears filled her eyes, but she didn't say much; mostly she listened. Then she went into her room, shut the door, and didn't come out for at least an hour. After that, it amazed all of us that she then became the source of comfort for the rest of us.

I once heard that aging is like climbing a mountain. The view halfway up is better than the view from the base. The higher we climb, the more beautiful the vistas we see. The older I get, the more I understand about life, about myself, and about the world I live in.

I'll always remember the words of my first pastor, Walter Olsen. More than once he said, "I've never met a real saint who didn't have gray hair." He was reminding us that spiritual maturity took time and it involved growth. We receive the gray hair and wrinkles before we really solve many of the ongoing issues of life. Those who have aged in the best sense of the word have survived youth, and they have reached the age where they have learned enough to help guide those just starting to climb up the mountain.

Above all, this verse isn't to say that one age is better than another. If we live a life that honors God, we fulfill the promise of 16:31: "Gray hair is a crown of glory; it is gained in a righteous life." By simply living and following the commands of God, we have earned the right to speak and to share what we've learned.

Modern Proverb: *Every age is good. Gray hair is beautiful when worn by those who have lived right.*

Nagging Voices

*A continual dripping on a rainy day and a contentious
wife are alike; to restrain her is to restrain the wind or
to grasp oil in the right hand.*

Proverbs 27:15–16

I've really known only one woman who fits the picture of
the truly contentious woman. Not only was she the most
negative person I ever met, but she seemed to revel in finding the worst aspect of any situation and letting everyone
know. *Bitter* describes her closer than any word I know. Her
husband left her at least fifteen years before she started to
attend our church. But from her conversation, it sounded as
if he had "abandoned" her only months earlier. Everyone
who would listen heard of all her woes and the woes of the
whole world.

One year, a Sunday school class decided to pay all expenses
to send her son to summer camp. When I told her, she said,
"It's about time they did something for somebody. They could
have done it last year too."

She epitomizes the most negative personality and fits the
description in Proverbs. No one can stop her from complaining, just as no one can stop the constant dripping of rain. This
person is as unsteady as the wind and as slippery as oil. She
nags, argues, and irritates everyone.

This picture becomes clearer when we consider the period
known as the latter rains—three months of the year when it
rains night and day. In biblical times, the constant rain or the
gusty winds that wouldn't stop prevented people from working
outdoors and kept them confined, with their noisy complaining
filling every corner. As bad as it might be outside, the clanging
of words inside worsened the problem. The sages are saying,

"You can find shelter from any kind of storm, but you can't find safety from the nagging tongue."

Someone put it like this: "Rain wets the skin, but the incessant complaining goes all the way down to the bones."

Now that I've written all that, there are two things I want to point out. First, the example given is a woman. If we're not careful, we see this purely as a gender issue.

That's like saying, "All women are talkative and all men are taciturn," or "Only men abuse." Anyone who complains, groans, and moans endlessly is like listening to water slowly dripping—it's maddening and we want to escape.

Second, is it possible that this proverb may be saying something even more important than pointing to contentious people? Could it be that there is a biblical principle here we need to grasp—and it eludes most of us?

The concept I'm pushing toward is called *contentment.* This is one of the virtues of life that we often either ignore or look down on. In fact, if all of us were contented with our lives, Western commerce would slip into a tailspinning depression. That is to say, the Western way of life is built on discontent—on always wanting more, or seeking the better, newer, or prettier.

Contentment doesn't mean to lose interest in such things, but it becomes a matter of "It's all right if I have it, and it's okay if I don't get it."

Paul expresses the idea well in his letter to the Philippians. We think he wrote the letter while he was imprisoned in Rome. The believers at Philippi had sent him a gift, which he never identifies, but we assume it's money. He thanks them by writing, "I rejoice in the Lord greatly that now at last you have revived your concern for me; indeed, you were concerned for me, but had no opportunity to show it. Not that I am referring to being in need; for I have learned to be content with whatever I have. I know what it is to have little, and I know what it is to have plenty. In any and all circumstances I have learned the secret of being well-fed and of going hungry, of having plenty and of being in need" (Philippians 4:10–12).

There we have it. It's not owning or possessing; it's not doing without or being deprived—it's attitude. Paul expresses deep gratitude, as shown in other verses in the same chapter. But he has something to teach them—something that's effective because of his own personal conditions.

At the time of writing, if he was a prisoner in Rome, at worst that meant being in chains. At best, he would have been under house arrest. Regardless, he wasn't free to come and go or to make the choices we take for granted. In those days, being a prisoner meant he had to depend on others for his food, clothes, and other needs. Yet the man of faith says, "You know, it really doesn't make much difference what's going on outwardly. I'm inwardly at peace. That's enough."

That's a powerful concept for us—especially those of us in the modern world—not just to understand, but to accept as a desirable goal for ourselves. Contentment. This attitude says, "God, whether you give me little or much, you actually give me exactly what I need."

Without trying to speak against ambition or hard work (and he's not doing that), Paul is saying that our inner circumstances are far more important than our outer situations. Millionaires can lose everything in a single day. A house with all our possessions can burn. But who we are—that's what's solid. If our relationship with our loving Savior is right, we may not like what happens, but we can still rejoice and say, "Okay, God, you know best."

To convey this idea, Paul writes to his protégé Timothy, ". . . there is great gain in godliness combined with contentment, for we brought nothing into the world, so that we can take nothing out of it; but if we have food and clothing, we will be content with these. But those who want to be rich fall into temptation and are trapped by many senseless and harmful desires that plunge people into ruin and destruction" (1 Timothy 6:6–9). And then he goes on to write that oft-misquoted verse: "For the love of money is a root of all kinds of evil" (v. 10).

His point is this: Let's be thankful for what we have. We're alive and have food, shelter, and clothes to wear. If we appreciate what we have right now, we're in good standing with God.

This message reminds me of my favorite piece of doggerel, which I first read at age sixteen: "As you wander on through life, brother, whatever be your goal, keep your eye upon the doughnut, and not upon the hole." To me, it was a way of saying, "Look at what you have and be thankful. Don't focus on what you don't have or what you want to have. Be thankful for what you have now."

Modern Proverb: *The complaining and dissatisfied are miserable people, and they also make others miserable.*

Good Wives

A good wife is the crown of her husband, but she who brings shame is like rottenness in his bones.

Proverbs 12:4

My wife has taught me a lot through the years of our marriage. Watching how she deals with people and situations has helped me. For example, when she's asked to do something she doesn't want to do, she's able to look the person in the eye, smile, and say, "No, thank you," and doesn't feel compelled to give a reason. I'm still not good at doing that, but I've learned to say, "No, I wouldn't be comfortable doing that."

I've rubbed off on her as well. I've helped her to be a little more outgoing, to enjoy social and recreational activities a little more.

That's the way marriage works—each person affects and changes the other. Sometimes those changes improve one person's personality, but there are instances when it goes the other way. So whether improving or tearing down, any behavior affects both people in the marriage relationship.

In this proverb, the word translated as *good* is more accurately translated as *strong* or *firm* and refers to strength of character or a woman's ability as a housewife and her integrity as a woman. It's the same word Boaz used when he called Ruth "a worthy woman" (Ruth 3:11).

Such a woman not only brings honor and dignity to her husband, but also brings out the best in him. This wife strengthens her husband's social status, motivates and helps him to achieve his goals, and is delighted for him to be respected, honored, and loved.

In the same verse, the good wife contrasts sharply with

one who, through nagging and shameless behavior, makes her reputation worthless and brings disgrace to the family. The word translated as *brings shame* evokes the public humiliation brought upon an individual's spouse or parents because of immoral or foolish behavior. A wife's actions to bring shame could be anything from nagging to quarreling to adultery.

I used to hear statements such as "Behind every successful man is a supportive wife." That's essentially what this proverb says before it contrasts the nonsupportive wife. She brings shame on her husband that results in his failure. Ancient Hebrews may not have known much about bone cancer, but the "decay" or "rottenness" suggests physical disease. The idea here is that she's like a form of decay that touches the bones and continues to gnaw away at his strength, marital happiness, morale, and the quality of his life.

One way to see it is to compare two women. The apostle Peter extols Sarah in her role as the best of wives of that time and culture: ". . . Sarah obeyed Abraham and called him lord" (1 Peter 3:6).

She's the opposite of Job's wife. After the death of their children and the loss of all their material possessions, sores on Job's body ran "from the sole of his foot to the crown of his head" (Job 2:7). His wife's true character shows when she screams to him at his lowest moment, "Do you still persist in your integrity? Curse God, and die" (v. 9).

A husband and a wife who work together reap success while those who work at odds with each other reap hardship and trouble.

If we can brush away the cultural issues of the day, it will help us understand the intent of this passage. The family arranged marriages, and sometimes the couple didn't know each other until the day of the wedding. Normally, love didn't form the basis of marriage. (Although Jacob's love for Rachel is evident, he apparently treated his other wife, Leah, with the proper honor and respect.)

The purpose for marriage, which goes all the way back to the Garden of Eden, said that God created a man and a woman to be joined together. Their purpose is to "become one flesh" (Genesis 2:24).

This makes an interesting form of arithmetic: One woman plus one man equals one full person. It's a way of acknowledging the weakness of the individual but the strength of the couple.

I'll give another personal example of how two become one. I do everything quickly. In fact, the Africans used to call me "Haraka," which means *swift* or *fast.* My wife tends to be slower and more methodical. Through our years together, she has speeded up a little and I've learned to slow down—a little anyway. I tended to be the person who was ready to get rid of anything we didn't need right then, and Shirley was the pack-rat. We have moderated each other.

Isn't that how a good relationship works? It's more than being a team effort; it involves two people functioning as one whole person. That doesn't mean one individual overwhelms the personality of the other. It's a merger, a blending, a growing together in which each smooths the rough edges of the other.

Failing to achieve this type of unity results in a sick marriage. While no one has a perfect marriage, the divine goal is still for both to work together so that they are one complete person. She adds the dimension of personality that he lacks, and vice versa. If we see this principle, it makes us more appreciative of God's wonderful plan for human marriage.

Modern Proverb: *A good wife makes a man better; and a good husband makes a woman better. Together they become one.*

Troubling Dads

Those who trouble their households will inherit the wind, and the fool will be servant to the wise.

Proverbs 11:29

When we lived in Kenya, my wife spoke at a women's convention. Polygamy is legal there, and one man came every day with his twenty-seven wives. In the three days, they didn't miss a single worship service or Bible study.

On the last day, the man came up to Shirley, his eyes filled with tears and obviously touched by what he had heard. "Today I have decided to become a Christian," he said. "My wives and I will all serve Jesus Christ from now on."

It was a great time of rejoicing, obviously, but it also troubled one of the new missionary women. "How can he decide for all his wives? Don't they have any voice in the matter?"

"Can he not speak for them?" Fibi, the African leader, asked. She didn't understand the problem. To her, the man's decision made sense. And to those who understood the older culture of Africa, it caused no problems. He was the husband, the head of that household, and he made decisions for all of them.

That kind of thing seems oddly out of focus with today's world. And it's amazing how little Proverbs has to say about the behavior of husbands and fathers. The proverbs speak many places about children and wives who trouble the husband. But apart from a few admonitions about not sparing the rod, it's assumed that the man will be a model father and husband. Of course, the proverbs were written by males, so they would tend to see things from their point of view.

The proverbs accepted the father as the center of the home. It was understood that the greatest threat to the stability of the family was undermining the father's authority. If his family position was undermined, so was his standing in the community and, with it, the position of the entire family.

Without arguing about male leadership in our modern world, we can learn an important lesson if we see these instructions through the eyes of those who received them.

These proverbs appeared at a time when, ideally, the father was the power and the center of the family. If he was lazy or foolish, or strayed from his family, not only did he lose, but everyone in the family suffered. He was responsible not only for himself, but for the well-being of the family—which included far more responsibility than providing a livelihood.

The story of Achan in Joshua 7 provides us with one way to understand this principle. When the people of Israel conquered Jericho, God told them to take nothing—to destroy everything, including animals, women, and children. Everything at Jericho was to become a holy offering to God. One man, however, took gold and clothing, and God showed Joshua who did it. The man, Achan, was stoned to death for this serious crime.

But it's even more significant than the death of one man. The people not only destroyed the stolen goods and brought Achan in front of everyone to be stoned, but "his sons and daughters, with his oxen, donkeys, and sheep, and his tent and all that he had" (Joshua 7:24) were to be stoned as well.

Just before killing all of them, Joshua asked Achan: "Why did you bring trouble on us?" (v. 25) Notice that he said "on us," making it obvious that it wasn't one man's sin and that the entire family would have to pay for his crime.

Destroying Achan, his family, and his livestock illustrates an important principle in ancient Israel—and something we tend to overlook or deny: *Our actions affect others.*

After the downfall of Jericho, the Israelites went to their next battle—against a tiny city called Ai. They were defeated, and thirty-six soldiers died. When Joshua cried out to God, he learned that the entire nation had been defeated *because of one man's sin.*

They were God's chosen people and had vowed to live by the conditions of the covenant. This horrible incident is abhorrent to our way of thinking today, but it made sense in that culture. It was a way of saying, "You *are* your neighbor's keeper. You are more than one isolated individual. Whatever you do affects everyone within the nation."

The story ended with the death of Achan and his family and cattle—every one of them stoned to death and then burned. It's not a pleasant story, and the horror of it may easily blind us to the principle of that day. It's called responsibility. It's also called accountability. This story shows the effect of the action of one man. By committing just one evil, deliberately disobedient deed, he changed the lives of everyone close to him. Innocent people died because of his sin.

We aren't alone. We belong to each other. With the Internet and technology, we're beginning to realize that we live in a global village—a small world where we affect, and are affected by, one another. We are connected. Our actions and our attitudes go far beyond our personal boundaries.

Those may sound like frightening words, but think of all the good we could bring about in the world by healthful and positive actions!

Modern Proverb: *Fathers who cause trouble or behave stupidly not only hurt themselves but their families as well. In fact, this is true about everyone.*

Wanting the Ultimate

But he who commits adultery has no sense; he who does it destroys himself.

Proverbs 6:32

"I really wanted love, but I settled for sex."

I had been the pastor of an Atlanta southside church for three years before Marie said those words. A member of the mutual-help group Parents Without Partners, she had come to our church, where she felt accepted and brought many of her single friends with her.

Five years a widow, Marie had had a series of short-term affairs with men, and she was tired of the casualness of sex. "It's such a boring routine. After introductions and a few bantering words between us, almost every man I meet then asks, 'Your place or mine?'"

By her sad confession, Marie opened my naive eyes to the area of sex outside of marriage. Today, it seems to be assumed that when male meets female and they spend time together, sex is an acceptable part of the relationship.

Even though it seems so casual and "everyone in the singles' scene does it," Marie put her finger on the issue when she said what she wanted and what she felt she had settled for.

Marie, a loving, giving person herself, wanted affection, compassion, and caring from a man. In short, she wanted a healthy relationship. After a few bad experiences and feeling she couldn't have what she wanted most, she became as promiscuous as the men she dated.

As I've continued to think about the growing acceptance of sexual activity outside of marriage, I see two significant factors at work. But first, I want to make my position clear.

I wouldn't call sex sacred, but I would say that it belongs in a sacred relationship. My understanding of marriage comes from Paul's words to the Ephesians in 5:21–33, where he compares the husband-and-wife relationship to the church and Christ. He quotes from Genesis 2:24, which describes how a man leaves his family, joins his wife, and the two become one. That's also a picture of our relationship with our Savior.

Sexual intercourse is sometimes referred to as "knowing," as in Genesis 4:1, 17. The *knowing* expresses the ultimate self-giving of one person to another. The only permanent, voluntary social relationship in our lives involves marriage. (Yes, people divorce, but we assume that when they marry, the intention is for the relationship to last as long as both are alive.) We can't choose our parents, siblings, or offspring, but we can select our mate.

This mate, by God's intention, enables us to become complete. That's what so many people seem to miss. When we join with another person, it's as if we're exploring the relationship to find the missing parts of ourselves. That other one—the partner we choose—provides that which we lack.

We can see this fairly easily by looking at couples. People often say that opposites attract, but I don't think that's quite right. I like to think that those who help us on our journey toward becoming a full person attract us. The goal, then, of marriage is for two people to work toward becoming one—a unity. God said it in Genesis 2:24, and Paul repeats it in Ephesians 5:31.

Now that I've stated my position, I see sex outside of marriage as essentially an act of selfishness. Whether male or female, it says, "My desires are more important than anything else. I want self-satisfaction and I want it now and I want it from you."

Surveys over the years have shown that one major reason many teenage girls have sex with their boyfriends is the social pressure. By removing social taboos and flaunting it in films, TV, and books, we have made this ultimate and most intimate act a shoddy act of selfishness.

"If you really love me," the aggressor often says. Those

words take the spotlight off selfishness and put it on the other. Nice manipulation.

The other issue I see is that of instant gratification—which is also a form of selfishness. "I want it and I want it now."

We live in a world where we want everything now and seem to feel as if it's our right to have it. No matter how commonly accepted sexual activity is outside of marriage, it makes me feel a bit sad for those who settle for what they can get from another instead of holding out for what they truly want.

Modern Proverb: *Too many settle for sexual gratification when they really want to be loved.*

Cheery Medicine

A cheerful heart is a good medicine, but a downcast spirit dries up the bones.

Proverbs 17:22

Rita died last year. She was one of those people who was constantly sick with something. Her husband, although not a difficult person, is what I would call dour. I think I saw him smile once.

A sad couple, but even sadder is their daughter, who's now in her forties and hasn't had a well day since she was a teenager. The accident-prone son has visited the hospital's ER so often that the staff call him by name.

My purpose isn't to judge that family; however, I suspect that the son and daughter aren't sickly for purely physical reasons. My theory is that quite early in life they picked up the spirit—the negativity—in their home. If my thinking is correct, then those two started out life disadvantaged—they were already primed for ill health.

What might life have been in that family if the attitude had been different? What would it have been like if the father had tried to be optimistic about life? What if Rita had shown a more positive attitude?

Which brings me to this question: How important is our attitude? Especially in the family, how important should we consider the way we come across to our children, to our mates, and to visitors? My answer: It has everything to do with health.

Modern science has recently caught on and affirmed that the mind is one of the best healers we have. If we have a positive attitude, we feel better. A dozen surveys have shown that hospital patients who have cheery friends and a support system recover better and go home sooner.

94

When Dr. Jan Kuzma and I wrote our book, *Live 10 Healthy Years Longer*, one of the points we wanted to make—which is well documented—is that the more positive we are, the more it influences how we feel and strongly enhances our general health. We document the importance of an optimistic attitude and the research showing that even when they get sick, those with cheerful attitudes recover more quickly.

When we were writing the book, Jan frequently quoted, "A cheerful heart is a good medicine." He believes it, lives it, and says his extraordinary health results from a positive attitude.

This cheery medicine shows through such simple things as smiling, laughing, speaking kind words, encouraging others, and learning to see things positively.

My friend Amy is eighty-three years old and in good health—each week she clogs, ballroom-dances, and has the energy of most women half her age. The other day I called her and asked, "How are you?"

"I'm blessed," she said.

That's the kind of cheery medicine that keeps her healthy.

In short, anything we can do for ourselves and for each other to turn us toward the positive makes us healthier.

This truth became clear to me when I was the pastor of a growing church. At one point, we attracted a plethora of depressed people—most of them on medication. I didn't know much about depression, but I listened and asked questions; I wanted to learn about these people.

One of them, Nancy, sat in my office and talked about her depression. I don't recall saying much, but I kept asking questions and she told me some of the causes and results of her depression. After perhaps fifty minutes, she smiled as she got up to leave. "I feel much better," she said. At the door, she paused and added, "You've helped me so much."

That incident helped me focus on what I had done. It seemed like so little, but I listened and smiled and encouraged her. Simple, perhaps obvious things, but they were, from a biblical perspective, cheery medicine.

The ancient people might not have had our medical information and technology, but they keenly observed human behavior. One of their observations linked attitude to health. They realized that an upbeat attitude promotes health and that a downcast, discouraged spirit works against recovery. The CEV translation of the proverb—"If you are cheerful, you feel good; if you are sad, you hurt all over"—says this well.

The contrast in Proverbs 17:22 isn't between joy and sorrow—because we all feel those emotions at times—but focuses on our disposition toward life. Those with glad attitudes are cheerful and have positive and optimistic outlooks on life, and they find things to be happy about. When they smile, it's infectious. Such dispositions pay dividends in healthy bodies.

If we're positive and optimistic, not only does it enhance our health, but what a difference we can make in our children or those we live with. We can bring into our homes a burst of permanent sunshine.

The proverb also mentions the sorrowful heart—those who are morose, anxiety-laden, guilt-laden, or pessimistic. They're the people who constantly find something to complain about. They're not fun to be around because they have a litany of complaints, groans, aches, and protests about life. This proverb says it and research confirms it—downcast dispositions pay off in bad health.

The kind of cheerfulness that brings health to the body and strength to the spirit doesn't come naturally for most of us—it's a quality we cultivate. It's easy to fall into the grumbling pattern and sometimes difficult to look on the bright side of life. Hard, yes. Impossible? No. That's what makes us humans unique. We can change.

We're more than a body. We're also our thoughts and emotions. If we focus on our body—especially our health or lack of it—we tend to view good health as an end in itself and encumber ourselves with doing all the right things to be physically strong.

I've worked at being more positive in my attitude about myself and about others. Two colds in the past twenty years are the worst physical ailments I've suffered. Part of that comes from the genes, I'm sure, but it's also because of a daily exercise program that I enjoy, and I eat in healthy ways. But I also believe that the more I cultivate *an optimistic attitude,* the healthier I am—the attitude that seeks the good and minimizes the bad.

I'll give two instances of things I've done to help bring that about.

First, years ago, I determined not to blame, only to accept. It wasn't always easy, but I can say that I'm not a blamer.

Second, I've been learning to handle problems better. I've kept a journal since 1971. Although I rarely look back, while working on another book and wanting to be sure I remembered correctly, I opened my journal for 1979. I had written about problems, mentioned names of those involved, and poured out my frustration or anger or whatever the emotion was.

As I read one entry, I honestly didn't remember it. In fact, I had written the names of two people who were giving me problems. But today, I have no idea who they are. Strange, isn't it, that at the time, I devoted so much energy to such hassles?

I also recorded my annual cold and a lot of problems with my allergies. (For the record, I began to change my lifestyle and attitude, and for the past decade, I haven't needed medication for my allergies.) I changed my attitude and that changed my health.

Modern Proverb: If we embrace a healthy, cheery attitude, we give ourselves effective medicine. A bad attitude weakens us physically.

Hardened

Happy is the one who is never without fear, but one who is hard-hearted will fall into calamity.

Proverbs 28:14

One who is often reproved, yet remains stubborn, will suddenly be broken beyond healing.

Proverbs 29:1

I don't know why I still remember after all these years, but I've never forgotten Dan. We were classmates together in my second year at a small Christian college in the Midwest. I liked Dan, but his behavior bothered me. For one thing, it was a college where we signed statements that said we wouldn't do certain things, such as smoke or drink alcohol. We also agreed to "abstain from all appearance of evil" (a direct quote from 1 Thessalonians 5:22, KJV).

I didn't live in the men's dorm, so I didn't know about his behavior there, but I knew about him away from the college. Dan worked part time in one of the Sears stores. A fellow student once remarked, "There isn't anything about the way he behaves that would have made anyone suspect he's a Christian, and especially not one who's preparing for the ministry."

I'll have to say this for Dan, though—he was good at repenting. We had chapel three days a week, and he regularly asked for prayer. Most times, he didn't explain the nature of his sinfulness, but he begged us to pray for him and for God to help him.

More than once, after chapel a small group of us gathered around and prayed for him. He cried and the tears flowed. Each time, we left feeling that Dan had gained a moral victory. But then, it wouldn't be long before he was back asking for prayer.

During the summer break, Dan traveled with a group for six weeks, representing the college, and appealing to students to make our college their choice.

Shortly after the new school year began, we learned about Dan and his repenting. During the summer, he had become sexually involved with another male student. After the administration learned of it (the other young man confessed), both were dismissed. I never heard from Dan again.

Over the years, however, I've thought about him and why he ended up in such a mess. In retrospect, I could see it coming. He was the kind of person who stretched the rules as far as he could. For instance, they had a curfew at the dorm—they didn't count people, but they locked out anyone attempting to enter after 11:00. Once he told me that he often waited right until curfew and a few times even came five minutes after everything was locked. (He arranged for someone to open the door from the inside and let him in.)

I could cite other on-the-edge things about Dan, but I think he was the kind of person this proverb speaks about—an individual who kept pushing grace. Perhaps that may not be the best theological phrasing, but Dan kept trying to get away with just a little bit more. He'd hand in assignments late—sometimes only an hour late, but more often a day and even a week past the deadline. Instructors would warn him, and he'd confess his failures in applying himself, and then do the same thing again.

I wouldn't call Dan a hypocrite. My understanding was that he was sincere *at the moment.* It was as if he accepted the spiritual lessons and guidance when he was with Christians or in the right atmosphere. But when he was on his own, Dan seemed to forget. Or maybe he hardened himself and eventually became calloused.

The last student to talk with Dan before he left the school said that she was sorry and she would pray for him. "Save your prayers for those who want them," he said.

This translation of Proverbs 29:1 reads "yet remains stubborn," but the words literally mean *hardens his neck.* This is like the difference between the palm tree and the oak. The palm tree survives the monsoons by bending to the strong winds, while the rigid oak, although strong enough to resist a lot of buffeting, can be suddenly broken—snapped—when severe storms rage.

Maybe, like a lot of us, Dan had begun to take God's grace for granted. God forgives. "After all, our Heavenly Father is in the forgiving business," someone said to me. That's true, but forgiveness also entails responsibility on our part. One of the implied things is that we fear God—that is, we revere our relationship with God so much we want to do nothing to jeopardize it in any way.

It also means that we don't want to repeat our wrongdoing. Asking forgiveness brings the heart of God into the picture.

I remember a story I heard years ago from my friend Max. A man's eighteen-year-old daughter had left home and moved in with three older, and rougher, young women. When Max saw the daughter one night and realized the lifestyle she was following, he asked her, "What would your dad say if he knew the way you're living?"

"He'd be there for me," she said.

"Are you sure? Maybe his heart would be too broken."

The daughter made some caustic remark and ran off with her friends. Nearly a month passed before she returned home. "I couldn't really enjoy my life after Max talked to me," she told her dad. "I kept thinking about you and how hurt you must be."

The father and daughter had a tearful reunion, and the story makes me think a little of our approach to God. If we bear in mind whatever we do or say touches the heart of our Heavenly Father, how then do we behave?

Proverbs 28:14 speaks of the blessing of being filled with awe or godly fear. Like others, this proverb presents the contrast: "but one who is hard-hearted will fall into calamity." These words stand as a warning to those who go astray or deviate from a total commitment. One translation puts it this way: "If you keep being stubborn after many warnings, you will suddenly discover that you have gone too far" (CEV).

How do we know when we've gone too far? No one knows. But isn't it better to play it safe and be sensitive to God's will?

To do whatever we can to gain the blessings and smile of God? Isn't it better to seek to stay close to God?

Modern Proverb: *Those who live close to God's commands are blessed; those who stray and harden themselves are the true losers in life.*

Accusing Others

Do not slander a servant to a master, or the servant will curse you, and you will be held guilty.

Proverbs 30:10

Martha, the supervisor, listened to accusations against Judy by two women who worked in the same department. As was later brought out, Martha actually encouraged the two women to speak to her against Judy. Finally, she thought she had enough evidence and tried to terminate Judy. The case backfired, because she had built her case on unsupported stories by the two women. This story has what I would call a happy ending. Martha was fired and Judy replaced her. The accuser ended up the cursed one.

Life doesn't always work out like that, and yet this proverb speaks about a general principle. Although it's not clear in the Hebrew text who slanders and who gets cursed, this translation probably has it correct—the servant who gets slandered will curse the false accuser, and that false accuser will be punished.

To understand what the sages were saying, let's first look at the historical context. It's a message about servants, and in those days, they were often considered part of the family, even though they were usually slaves. If anyone accused the servant, the poor wretch would curse the accuser. Quite likely, this happened more often than we might think, and especially in a culture where slaves had no one to stand up for them. Even so, those who falsely accuse will be held guilty. The implication is that the community would learn of the wrongful words, and neighbors and family would shame the accuser.

Second, if we take this proverb and apply it to a broader world, what does it say to us? If nothing else, it reminds us of a lack of compassion that causes us to judge others. Even though we may not call it judging, when we speak harshly against others or accuse them of specific attitudes and motivations, we *are* judging them.

Too often the accusations—especially false or imagined ones—say more about the accusers than they do the alleged wrongdoer. For example, think of David in his younger years. He served under King Saul, and from everything we read, he faithfully performed his duties. During his years of running from Saul, David never retaliated. On two occasions, when he could have killed the king, he refused to harm him.

After the second time David had spared the king's life, he yelled to Saul from a safe distance and told him that he had spared his life. Saul said, "I have done wrong . . . I have been a fool, and have made a great mistake" (1 Samuel 26:21). Despite admitting the wrong he had done to his servant, King Saul didn't stop pursuing David. He knew that one day the younger man would take over the throne, and he tried to hold onto his kingdom and to destroy his enemy.

King Saul finally died in battle. The point I make is that Saul made wild accusations against David. Had it not been for divine protection, David would have died young.

Elsewhere I've mentioned Haman, the prominent man in the Persian court who schemed to kill Mordecai the Jew. Apparently, he was consumed with hatred, and killing Mordecai and ridding the empire of all Jews filled his thoughts. Haman had workers build a gallows about seventy-five feet high to hang his enemy. Despite the wicked man's plan, the king exalted Mordecai and hanged Haman on that same gallows.

In both illustrations I've presented—Saul and Haman—they accused others. The desire to destroy their enemy—who had done them no harm—became an obsession. In the end, the hearts and motives of the two accusers led to their destruction.

Someone said it this way: "Those who take the most pleasure in finding fault are usually those who can least bear the accusation themselves." The way I like to think of it is that the things we speak the most vigorously against may point to our very weaknesses.

"If you listen closely to what people are against, you often learn their great weaknesses," said one of my seminary professors. He didn't mean it as an infallible rule, but he observed that those who screamed loudly for certain causes were actually reflecting something about themselves.

Many years ago I heard an audiotape by the then-popular writer Keith Miller. Much of his early writing was about being honest and truthful. The interviewer asked, "Why do you speak so much about honesty?"

"I suppose it's because basically I'm not an honest person," he said.

He was more aware of his shortcomings than most of us. It was as if he spoke about the need for honesty as part of the way to bring about more integrity in his own life.

I've also seen this from a humorous viewpoint. I had a friend named Diane who had one quality that bothered me—she gossiped about everybody. I figured she talked about me to others. One day I mentioned a woman named Vera who went to the same church as Diane. "Do you know her?" I asked.

"Oh, yes, I certainly do, and she's the biggest gossip peddler there."

I turned away, afraid that I might laugh in Diane's face. It's easy, I thought, to accuse others of the things that trouble us. I wonder if that's not part of the implied message of this proverb. Too often, then, when we accuse, expose, or even suspect other people, we may be pointing at ourselves without being aware where that finger points.

Years ago, when I said some rather unkind things about someone and how much he irritated me, a friend said, "Ever drive down the highway and the bright lights from an oncoming car blind you?" When I said I had, he said, "Maybe that's what's going on here."

I didn't like to admit it, but my friend told me what I needed to hear.

One final thought. Like the servants in ancient Israel, many of those we condemn or accuse may not be able to defend themselves—especially if they don't know what we're accusing them of in secret. The principle, however, still applies. That is, we're guilty.

Modern Proverb: *Take no pleasure in finding fault with others. The fault we find with others may reflect our own shortcomings.*

PART THREE

Living and Working with Others

Soft Answers

A soft answer turns away wrath, but a harsh word stirs up anger.

Proverbs 15:1

My wife's mother, who had already been teaching thirty years, gave me a practical piece of advice before I began to teach sixth grade in a public school. She quoted this very proverb about a soft answer turning away wrath and added, "Parents will come in angry and scream at you. If you can remain calm, you'll win them over."

Two weeks after classes began, I faced my first test. The girl's name was Florence, and I remember only that her previous teacher had warned me to expect frequent visits from her mother to complain and to tell me off.

Florence's mother burst into the room while the children were still filing out at the end of a school day. She didn't even wait until she got to my desk but started to yell from the doorway.

The rudeness of that woman, I thought, and I was ready to explode with a verbal blast. Then I remembered Mom's advice. I stood up, walked toward her, and held out my hand. "Hello, I'm Mr. Murphey. What can I do for you?"

Her startled look lasted a few seconds before she relaunched her tirade. I waited until she paused and then said, "Please sit down. You look as if you're under a lot of stress." I led her to a chair.

"You discriminate against my Florence. You make her look like an idiot in class." (Florence was one of the poorest students in the class.) She railed on for quite a while.

"You know, I wish all parents cared as much about their

children's education as you do. This must have meant a lot to you to make this long drive to see me." Inside I was raging, but I forced myself to stay calm, and silently I kept repeating, "A soft answer turns away wrath."

"I know Florence isn't very bright," she said, "and it's so hard for us. Her younger brother is in second grade and she can't read as well as he can." Then she began to cry.

Florence's mother and I never got to be friends, and she still stormed into my classroom three more times that year. Each time, I quoted the proverb to myself. Each time, calmness came over me and I was able to listen to that sad woman instead of retaliating or silently raging.

When I think of the origin of this proverb, I can imagine that the sages of Israel observed people and the way they handled anger. They saw that an enraged person stirred up anger in others. If one man screamed loud, harsh words, the other person probably responded with louder and angrier words. Obviously, the violent words escalated into violent actions.

That picture sounds rather modern, doesn't it? It *is* timeless, because people haven't changed much through the centuries.

Here's a biblical example. In the early days of Israel before they had a king, Gideon championed the cause of the people and defeated the attacking Midianites. However, some of the men of the tribe of Ephraim didn't get called by Gideon to fight and angrily confronted the hero. "'What have you done to us, not to call us when you went to fight against the Midianites?' And they upbraided him violently" (Judges 8:1).

How did Gideon handle it? With the soft answer, of course. He spoke appeasing words, and the Bible says, "When he said this, their anger against him subsided" (v. 3).

That event happened centuries ago. Here's a modern example.

I'm no expert on anger, and it's something I've struggled with all my life. But I learned something useful in dealing with it. It also ties in with the soft answer. My event happened over lunch with a casual friend back in the early days of computers, when Macintosh and IBM computers couldn't read each other.

Harold was a Mac user—no, more correctly, he was a Mac

zealot. One day he yelled at me for being so stupid because I hadn't bought a Mac. For a couple of minutes, he raged. I couldn't understand what had set him off. I had simply said, "I started with an IBM clone and I've learned it. It works for me."

His voice had reached a high pitch and he started telling me that I was too stupid not to realize the superiority of the Mac. Abruptly he stopped. "Why am I so mad at you?" he asked.

"I don't have any idea."

He stared out the window for at least a minute before he said, "I guess you just happened to be here. I'm so angry with my boss, I'm almost ready to quit." Then he unloaded about what he considered his mistreatment and the bad morale in the office.

"You know, Harold, we're seldom angry about what we think we're angry about," I said. Just as those words popped out of my mouth, I had a moment of deep insight. Yes, I thought, that's how anger works. The experts call it misplaced anger.

The fury that overwhelms common sense happens all the time—the road-raged driver, the rude customer in the checkout line, or the irate taxpayer. Sometimes people embrace causes and we hear the rage in their voices and their gestures. They're angry, and all too often they're not expressing their feelings to the right people or the right causes.

Maybe a quiet answer carries so much power because it stops wrath from falling on the wrong object or person.

One friend, whom I admired for his calmness, said, "I find it helps if I think of enraged people as being crazy and out of control. If I fight back, I make them crazier. If I think of them as temporarily sick, then I want to offer help. I can do that by demonstrating the kind of behavior I want them to have." He smiled before he said, "Most of the time it works."

Yet our culture teaches us that we're weak wimps if we don't stand up. I don't advocate being doormats for anyone, but standing up may be the way to get knocked down. Any fool can scream, yell, or insult. It takes far more character to meet any angry person with calmness and to respond in a soft voice.

It helps if we remember that once we erupt in front of

another person, our words are out there. They can't ever be retracted. We can repent and ask forgiveness, but we can't take back those words.

Modern Proverb: *Anyone can grow angry. We're most helpful when we respond to anger with soft words.*

Lazy Benefits

The lazy person does not plow in season; harvest comes, and there is nothing to be found.

Proverbs 20:4

The craving of the lazy person is fatal, for lazy hands refuse to labor.

Proverbs 21:25

In college, I learned to take excellent notes in all the lectures. Immediately after classes finished, I rushed home and typed up my notes, and at the same time, I added any other information I remembered.

During my first year of graduate school, another student named Richard asked if he could borrow my notes for a particular course. Most of my classmates knew about my notes and would occasionally borrow one day's lecture. Richard asked if he could have the whole set because he had missed a number of classes. "I've been sick," he said, although he never specified what was wrong with him.

We were a week away from finals, and though I didn't know Richard well, I felt sorry for him. "I'll loan you my notes, but I must have them back tomorrow," I said. I carried a large three-ring notebook with all my class notes. I started to pull out the pages he wanted, but he said, "Look, I'm in a hurry. Loan me the whole thing and I'll give your notebook back first period in the morning."

I handed him the notebook. The next morning at the beginning of my first class, Richard returned my notes and thanked me. That would have ended the story except that word got back to me that Richard received a B average in three of his classes, even though he had attended less than half of the lectures. I didn't connect my notes with his grades—not then.

Because I worked hard all during the semester, read extra material, and made notes on that as well, I had produced an extremely valuable set of papers. In fact, I usually knew the material so well, I had no problems with finals and always did extremely well.

"Bet you're proud of Richard," Jerry Davis said. He was my best friend at seminary, but he spoke sarcastically. "He got three B's this semester because of your notes."

"No, that's not true," I said. "He only used the notes from one class."

Then Jerry told me differently. He worked part time at the library on a scholarship. When Richard came in, Jerry watched him copy all my notes at the photocopier. He also made copies for two of his frequently-absent-from-class friends. "You know where they studied? They went down to the basement of the library and stayed there each night going over your notes until the library closed. Then they studied at Don's apartment [one of the others who lived off campus]."

Jerry's words shocked me. Then I realized Richard had stolen all my material—instead of using notes from one class, he had used them for the three classes we both took. He hadn't asked for permission to copy or share them.

"But he's got physical problems," I said to Jerry. "I suppose I could overlook it this time."

Jerry laughed. "You know what his problem is? He's too lazy to get out of bed in the morning. He watches TV until about 2:30 in the morning and then he can't get up to go to class."

I didn't want to believe what Jerry told me. Yet the more I thought about it and the more I pieced together little things I'd heard around the campus, I knew it was true. I also learned that Richard had never gotten a single grade above C before he used my notes.

For me, this incident illustrates the truly lazy person— someone who simply refuses to work and then tries to justify such behavior. In Proverbs we read many statements against the lazy.

Some of them are intended to make us laugh or scorn the lazy. For instance, the lazy person finds every possible excuse not to go to work. The flimsiest is that he won't leave his house because "there is a lion in the road!" (Proverbs 26:13). That's like our saying today, "I don't want to go to work today because there will be at least one traffic fatality today and I don't want it to be me."

In ancient cultures—and probably in most cultures until recently—being lazy was the worst label to hang on anyone. Life, often precarious and difficult, meant that everyone had to work and carry part of the load. In the agrarian culture of the Old Testament, everyone had to be mentally and physically able to work effectively to produce food to carry them through the next year.

The various proverbs present different facets of the simple principle that hard work at the right times is essential for success and for gaining respect from others. But there have always been those who want to sleep through the work periods. Today, they probably don't use the excuse of wanting to sleep, and who wants to be labeled lazy? They have a myriad of excuses. One of the best is that they have too much to do—and they never explain what "too much" is. Or they talk about holding back because of frustration or inefficiency in their company. The single greatest excuse in the commercial world comes from those who claim unjust treatment by their companies and then ask, "Why should I work hard when they treat me this way?"

As I look at the principles of these lazy-person proverbs, they come down to one thing: The lazy make the basic error of expecting to achieve without doing the necessary work. When I wrote that, I thought how utterly silly it sounded, but I believe it's true.

One of the most popular excuses today is that we want "quality living" and aren't willing to go without that. That may sound all right, but serious reflection makes us ask, "Is it?" Maybe it's a way of saying we want our desires fulfilled but we're unwilling to work hard enough to bring them about.

In her recent *USA Today* article titled "Diets, Scales, Fat-Loss Books," Nancy Heilmich reported on a fifty-two-year-old Dallas man who had struggled with his weight for years. The man said that learning to eat right robbed him of a "quality of life."

"As for exercise, he says, 'Forget that. Who has time for it?'" He also commented that he'd rather die than go on a fat-free diet. (No diet I know of demands people go fat-free, and even the most strenuous usually allow 10 percent fat.) This sounded like a person who excused his lack of change by blaming something else. Isn't that characteristic of the lazy? What truly lazy person ever says, "Yes, I ought to work harder, but I'm just too lazy to do it"?

Or take the matter of "a quality retirement." We want that, of course, but if we save our money, goes the argument, we can't enjoy the quality of life now. That kind of statement comes from those who are heavily in debt, despite the amount of money they earn, and who usually have their next paycheck spent before it arrives.

Maybe that's the real problem with those called lazy by Proverbs. They want all the good things of life—and who doesn't?—but they don't want to pay for it. They're like Richard, who wanted good grades, but he didn't want to study hard. Or like the Dallas man who found a variety of excuses because eating right interfered with his quality of life.

Maybe the best we can do is to remind ourselves that we must pay a price for everything we get. Desires get us no place unless we're willing to do something ourselves.

"God helps those who help themselves" isn't a biblical verse, but maybe it ought to be.

Modern Proverb: *We get exactly nothing for nothing. If we want the good things in life, we have to work for them.*

Don't Blame Me!

Crooked minds are an abomination to the LORD, but those of blameless ways are his delight. Be assured, the wicked will not go unpunished, but those who are righteous will escape.

Proverbs 11:20–21

"Well, I didn't do it," my older daughter said.

"I didn't either," my younger daughter said.

"I wasn't around," my son said.

It wasn't a big thing. Someone had left an empty glass on the front porch. I felt myself getting upset, because one of them was lying. The glass had not been there an hour earlier, and no one else had come to our house. My wife was gone, and I knew I didn't leave it there.

Just as I opened my mouth to start the interrogation, I realized that I was repeating a pattern set in my childhood. The pattern was to discover a misdeed and then to stay on the case until we discovered the guilty person. It might take an hour, but that didn't matter. In this case, I could just as easily pick up the glass myself and take it inside. As I looked at my kids, I thought, *It really isn't important to discover the identity of the guilty party.*

"Okay, whoever left the glass, please take it back to the kitchen." I turned and walked inside. My younger daughter picked up the glass, grinned, and took it inside.

A small incident? Of course, but it taught me something quite powerful: No one wants to be blamed, especially the guilty.

I understand that part, but I've always had trouble with the idea of the Bible calling us *blameless.* Maybe it's because I came from a family where finding the guilty person seemed always to be of great importance. Whenever anything went wrong, we had to find the one who had violated family law. Or maybe it's just because I rarely feel blameless about my life.

Yet it's a good word, and we find it several times in the New Testament. For instance, Paul writes to the Philippians and reminds them that God is at work in them, and he makes it clear that part of the divine purpose is "so that you may be blameless and innocent, children of God without blemish in the midst of a crooked and perverse generation, in which you shine like stars in the world" (Philippians 2:15).

Another reason the word *blameless* has troubled me is that because, even though I know differently, my mind equates blameless with perfection: ". . . but those of blameless ways are his delight." Once I remind myself that the two words don't mean the same thing, the terms fit a little easier. *Blameless* then means that God forgives when we confess and no longer counts us guilty. Even more exciting, God wants us to be blameless, and we do that by being free of known sin. I didn't have to be part of the church very long before I learned to quote: "If we confess our sins, he who is faithful and just will forgive us our sins and cleanse us from all unrighteousness" (1 John 1:9).

Blameless, then, doesn't mean we have to be good enough or work hard enough to get divine blessings. It's a matter of our accepting God's forgiveness. Or maybe it's more accurate to say it means learning to accept grace.

That's been a tough bit of practical theology for me. I've preferred to earn or deserve what I get, but grace says, "You deserve to be punished. However, instead you get hugged."

Intellectually, I've had no trouble with that. Emotionally, it's been difficult for me to grasp. Yet when we admit our inability to make ourselves good enough, the loving and compassionate Savior says, "Ah, at last, you got the message."

We've known all along that Jesus Christ—the one who was totally blameless and innocent—died for us, the guilty, flawed, and sinful. It's quite an emotional jump to say, "Once I was lost but now I'm found; I was blind but now I see." Yet that's grace at work.

It reminds me of something that happened when I was about

ten years old. Mel, my brother who was two years younger, got away with a lot of mischievous things, and the rest of us kids knew it. One day I was particularly angry and I complained to my friend Chuck Baldwin. He listened and didn't say much—he knew Mel.

A few days later, Chuck and I were playing, and he said something about Mel and proceeded to tell me how rotten he was. I felt anger rising in me. I punched Chuck hard in the stomach. "Don't you talk about him like that," I yelled.

My shocked friend looked at me. He reminded me of what I had said only days earlier. Then I said, "Yeah, I can blame him, but you can't. He's my brother!"

Isn't that how families work? Among ourselves we see the failures and shortcomings, but when an outsider tries to speak against a family member, we stand firm. Isn't that also how God works? God knows our imperfections, but when God speaks to the world about us, we're called blameless. As far as those outside the faith are concerned, we are everything God wants us to be.

The second line of this proverb reads: "Be assured, the wicked will not go unpunished . . ." I've often been troubled about the law of divine retribution, even though I know that ultimately the wicked get punished and the righteous get rewarded. We don't always see that happen in this life, although the Bible assures us that one day God will hold a final judgment, when all things will be made right.

This verse shows God's attitude toward the wicked—those who have cruel minds. The book of Proverbs emphasizes that everything the wicked think or do expresses rebellion against God, which is revealed in their behavior toward people. Some verses speak of God's unresponsiveness to the wickeds' futile religious practices, rejection of their sacrifices, and refusal to listen to their prayers, as in 15:8 ("The sacrifice of the wicked is an abomination to the LORD . . .").

In other proverbs, the sages sharply contrast good and evil or sin and righteousness. They also point out that those who live right please God.

If my life and lifestyle please God, it encourages me to know that I can expect divine blessings and guidance. A crooked mind is associated with twisted thinking, the kind of mindset that works against the right.

The phrase "be assured" comes from an untranslatable expression in Hebrew that literally means "hand to hand." It may refer to shaking hands—the idea of shaking hands on a promise—and may therefore mean "You can depend on it." Isn't that a nice way to think about God?

Modern Proverb: *Do right and be blameless. Do wrong and punishment follows.*

Shocking Love!

Hatred stirs up strife, but love covers all offenses
Proverbs 10:12

*Better is open rebuke than hidden love. Well meant are
the wounds a friend inflicts, but profuse are the kisses of
an enemy.*

Proverbs 27:5–6

I wish everyone had a friend like David Morgan. We've known
each other close to twenty-five years, and for the past decade
I've called him my best friend. David does one thing for me
that no other friend does: He rebukes me when I need it.

Maybe I need to make clear what I'm talking about. I can
find any number of people to tell me off, to make disparaging
remarks, or to blast me with cruel challenges when they don't
agree. David loves me enough to make me look at the truth
about myself. Such a message isn't always easy for me to
receive. I don't like hearing about my imperfections—but
sometimes I need to hear.

David and I talk on the phone regularly, but we try to have
a real face-to-face meeting every week. We sit and talk for at
least an hour—no agenda, no pressure, just time to be in each
other's presence and talk and listen.

We have a little game we've played for several years. It
started one day when David said something I didn't want to
hear. "I hate you!" I said.

He stared at me, totally shocked.

"I hate you for telling me the truth," I said. "Why do you
tell me things about myself that I don't want to know?"

David laughed and hugged me. "Because you really do
want to know."

This has now become our special "game," because even
after all the years of trust that we have built up between us, it

121

still embarrasses me when he forces me to face things about myself that I don't like to acknowledge. Sometimes it hurts me to see who I really am.

The relationship David and I share expresses the words of the second proverb well: "Well meant are the wounds a friend inflicts." Because our relationship is secure, we can openly rebuke each other. We've learned to speak frankly—not out of harshness or in judgmental tones, but out of love and desire for the growth of the other.

The first verse says, "Hatred stirs up strife, but love covers all offenses." It reminds me that we can hear the same message from someone who dislikes or belittles us and we respond differently. The words may be true, but they stir up resentment, and too often we respond in anger. The spirit of the speaker makes all the difference.

Most of us have known at least a few kisses from enemies. They flatter or repeatedly tell us they admire us and we're special to them. Yet something about the lack of warmth in the smile, the coldness of the eyes, or the hardness around the mouth enables us to discount their "kisses."

Their actions differ from the compassionate wounds of a friend. "The most important thing you can do for me is to tell me the truth about myself," David said to me years ago. "Even if I don't want to listen, tell me anyway."

When we speak frankly about a matter, sometimes it does hurt. But both of us know it's a temporary pain that brings healing and greater self-understanding. Another proverb says it this way: "Whoever rebukes a person will afterward find more favor than one who flatters with the tongue" (28:23).

Too many of us see the thing that needs telling, but we're afraid of hurting the other's feelings, so we remain silent. When we say nothing although the other needs to hear, that's denying our love because we don't express it. Once we realize that the most loving thing we can do is to speak the truth to the person we love, it deepens our relationship.

Too many so-called friendships are built on the foundation that we're always kind and sweet-tempered, and do nothing to upset the balance. We hesitate to bring a rebuke into the conversation because the friendship might crumble. Is that the kind of connection we really want?

True friendship is built on mutual respect, and that means we shouldn't allow false tenderness to dilute a serious obligation we have to others. Could Paul have answered to God for his love for Peter if he hadn't openly rebuked him? (See Galatians 2:11–14.)

Fear often holds us back. Perhaps we sense the other may not willingly hear our words. Further, we think, who wants such wounds? Yet true friendship means being faithful not just to our friend, *but also to ourselves.*

Years ago, a friend said something that hurt me deeply, but I needed his rebuke. "I care enough to confront you," he said. "If I say nothing, I'm encouraging you to continue in something that will eventually cause you a lot of grief."

Some of the most powerful experiences I've had with God have occurred when I've seen things about myself that I didn't like—and in a few instances detested. For example, I've never thought of myself as a proud person, but I have been. Not pride in the sense of lording it over people—my pride was in not needing help. After all, I had Jesus, so I could handle anything. Besides, I was the helper, the one who was able to be there for others, and who didn't mind being called at 2:37 in the morning. It took me a long time to realize my inner smugness that I didn't need to call people in the middle of the night with *my* problems.

Realizing that I needed to lean on others at times hurt to admit. In theory, I can see it all through the Bible. But those of us who have considered ourselves committed to God—maybe secretly superior to others who are less committed—find it just about impossible to say, "I need help." The more people told me how much I helped others, the more it played into that secret sense of pride.

When I understood that aspect of myself—and David was the scalpel in God's probing hand—I went into a depressive state for two days. At first I kept saying, "That can't be me, oh, dear Lord, that can't be me."

But it was. And I didn't like looking at my face in a spiritual mirror. Shame covered me. It was as if I had been the emperor showing off his new clothes. Surely everyone else saw my nakedness but me.

When I talked to my wife, she kissed me and held me. "Oh, yes, I know that," she said. Then her blue eyes stared right at me. "You've just learned it and you feel embarrassed. I've known it for years and I've loved you anyway."

And that's really the way God works as well, isn't it? God has always known and still loves us. And the same Great Benevolent Power really proves that love by sending David Morgans into my life as if to say, "Listen. This is my voice speaking to you. This open rebuke is really a tender message of love."

Along with that, I've realized something else. We hear those rebukes only when we're ready for them. In the recovery movement, they speak of being in a safe place. By that, they mean when we're secure—when we're ready and can cope— only then is God ready to send the message to us.

Modern Proverb: The people who truly love us tell us the truth about ourselves—even when we don't like what we hear.

Simply Believe

The simple believe everything, but the clever consider their steps.

Proverbs 14:15

"If you get an e-mail with the subject 'Honk if you love Jesus,' don't open it. It is a virus and it will destroy your computer." Like most people with e-mail, I received that message or a variation of it. I received such messages as "Sing if you love Jesus" or "Pray . . ." or sometimes I was supposed to honk if I loved peanut butter or apple pie or voted Republican.

At least ten people have forwarded on such messages. I figured out quite early it was a hoax. And there were other messages just as transparent. One of them said something about winning a thousand dollars from Microsoft if I responded immediately. Another tried to scare me by claiming that some kind of human-eating virus had infected the bananas imported from the Caribbean—as if the Food and Drug Administration wouldn't have alerted the nation.

All this is to illustrate how easily we get taken in. I mention the computer hoaxes and false-virus scares because those messages played on two things—naïveté and fear. Many people hardly know how to work on a computer, and fear paralyzes them—they worry they'll fry the internal mechanisms or erase all their data. Cruel people play on that fear.

In Proverbs, the simple are the naive who tend to believe anything they hear. From as early as Proverbs 1:4, the sages instruct readers in the ways of wisdom. They may have been writing to young people, the up-and-coming scholars who lacked experience of life and didn't know much about the false ways and wiles of the world. Such people were easily impressed or manipulated.

Life hasn't changed very much since then, has it? In the winter of 1999–2000, people all over the United States became alarmed over the flu bug. We began to hear words such as *epidemic* and *pandemic*. What we soon learned is that the Food and Drug Administration had okayed two flu-fighting drugs on which pharmaceutical companies spent millions to advertise. Many assumed we had an epidemic when, in reality, it was a normal flu season.

I can think of two reasons people believe things that common sense tells them aren't real. First, they readily accept whatever they hear as truth—especially if they hear it on TV or get it as e-mail. It simply doesn't occur to them to ask if such people can be trusted, or if the information is purely an advertisement. They don't think for themselves or weigh what they've heard. One translation puts it this way: "Don't be stupid and believe all you hear; be smart and know where you are headed" (CEV).

Second, they believe because they lack awareness of the consequences. It's as if they're driving down a highway with all kinds of detour signs that they ignore until it's too late. Faith is an admirable quality, but trust in the wrong person or things can turn to disaster.

"Just believe it!" I've heard people say. "Just trust God. Don't rely on your intellect." Such people seem offended when questioned or when I appeal to reason. My response to that is to quote the words of a poster that's displayed outside a Sunday school class at our church: "Jesus Christ came to take away our sins, not our minds."

Someone told me that the foolish are those "who are willing to drink anything set before them or they're like children who believe that anything sweet is good." The word *anything* distinguishes the foolish from being people of godly faith. Faith is desirable—when used in the right places and when it results in good.

We can play the role of the simple in many different ways.

Sometimes we're simply gullible, as this proverb points out. Because we trust certain individuals, whatever they say we assume is true, and we don't think to verify or clarify.

Sometimes we're overconfident of our own ability to understand and discern. In the Old Testament, Amaziah was king of Judah, the smaller Southern Kingdom that consisted of only two tribes. The Bible says he took counsel—assumedly from royal advisers—and sent a message to Joash and invited him to battle. He must have believed that he could defeat a nation five times stronger and larger than the kingdom of Judah.

Joash sent back an insulting response and added, "Your heart has lifted you up in boastfulness. Now stay at home; why should you provoke trouble so that you fall, you and Judah with you?" (2 Chronicles 25:19).

Amaziah wouldn't listen and insisted on a war. "Judah was defeated by Israel; everyone fled home. King Joash of Israel captured King Amaziah of Judah . . ." (vv. 22–23).

Sometimes it's just hasty action—the kind of people who lash out or jump into action with the slightest provocation. ". . . One who has a hasty temper exalts folly" (Proverbs 14:29).

So what does this proverb say to us today? It's certainly not urging us to be skeptical of everything we hear. However, the proverb does urge us to use common sense and to think before we decide or act.

Modern Proverb: *The gullible believe almost anything. Sensible people ask questions and look ahead before they believe.*

Rushing Fools

Like a dog that returns to his vomit is a fool who reverts to his folly.

Proverbs 26:11

You have just read the grossest illustration in the book of Proverbs—and maybe the sages meant it that way to make their point. It compares fools to dogs that go back and eat indigestible vomit—and it's disgusting to think about.

So what's the point? Simply that the most foolish thing we can do is return to that which previously harmed us. It means an unwillingness to learn from our mistakes.

Peter took this image from Proverbs and carried it to its worst expression. He discusses those who became believers in Jesus Christ and then turned back to their old ways. He says that once they've escaped the "defilements of the world" through faith in Jesus Christ, "they are again entangled in them and overpowered" (2 Peter 2:20–21). He goes on to add that it would have been better not to have known the way than, after having known, to turn back to their old ways. "It has happened to them according to the true proverb, 'The dog turns back to its own vomit'" (v. 22).

That's the extreme position that Peter presents. Apparently, some had professed faith, been active among other believers, and then renounced the faith. He says that instead of trying to sample the better things, such people revert to their old patterns.

Today, people don't live in such extreme situations, but like those of old, many still never learn from their mistakes. They keep making the same bad choices.

For example, my aunt by marriage had earned a well-deserved reputation for possessing one of the sharpest tongues around—one of those individuals who never had anything kind to say about anyone. Then, when she was in her late thirties, she had a conversion experience. Within a short time, everyone remarked about the change in her. The most remarkable thing was that she kept her mouth shut! When she did speak up, to the surprise of many, she actually spoke kindly.

For perhaps ten years she lived by the new image, and people liked her. She and her family became active in the church. Then, somewhere over the years, she reverted to her old ways. Maybe it was a gradual change—I'm not sure. I know only that the last few times I saw her before she died, I didn't enjoy being around her. As soon as anyone's name came up, she not only spoke negatively, she also opened her memory bank and brought out dusty records of things that person had done years earlier.

As I think of her, it reminds me of something a friend said about such people: "They're fools. They aren't usually malicious. They lack good sense. Their eyes aren't evil, only blind."

As I was reading about fools in Proverbs, I realized something. None of the sayings against such people are directed at the foolish ones themselves. Instead, they write to those who have to live with or around them. Wise living, then, means being able to accept people who never can get it figured out. Someone said fools don't know that they don't know that they don't know.

In reality, few people are total fools. For the purposes of instruction, the sages tended to exaggerate and divided people into categories of wise or foolish. Most of us aren't wise all the time, and the foolish may sometimes do wise things.

In terms of daily living, my concern is that once we know our bad habits or stupid actions and realize we can call on God's help in overcoming them, why do we persist in such behavior? Why do we go back and do the same foolish things again and yet again?

Earlier I mentioned my aunt with the wicked tongue. Here's another example, this one about a woman named Barbara, who had a near-death experience. I was then her pastor and she told me that the experience had changed her life, she was going to be different, and she needed to mend a lot of fences. Barbara promised not only to become active in church, but also "to find ways to help other people in need."

Barbara, who had been what I would have called a fairly self-centered woman, did change. She had been a demanding person who expected people to follow wherever she led. Some called her bossy and others called her a dictator, but she lost that bossiness and became cooperative and helpful.

People praised her for the change and told her how much they liked the new Barbara. And she smiled frequently, something I don't think she did much of before her near-death experience. She was a widow, and a new man came into her life. They began to talk seriously about the future.

Barbara's new life lasted maybe eight months. Then she crept back to her old ways. People resented her even more. Some spoke in quite unflattering words. The man in her life left her with these words (which Barbara told me herself): "I can't stand any more of your negativity."

I could cite other stories, and I'm sure we all know people like Barbara. Here's why I categorize her as a fool like those mentioned in the book of Proverbs. She had been delivered from an unhappy way of relating to others. People gave her wonderful feedback, accepted and encouraged her, and yet she still returned to her old ways.

How foolish. How stupid.

Isn't it gratifying that we don't do such things? We know our attitudes or words have hurt people, so we never speak harshly again. We never show impatience because we've learned the harm we've brought about.

Yes, it's nice to know that we're not like those people who revert to old, ugly, and quite stupid patterns. Or are we?

Maybe it's something we need to think about.

Maybe the sages were writing about people like us.

Modern Proverb: *Once we understand the right way to do things and begin to do them, we're fools if we go back to our former ways.*

Powerful Silence

One who spares words is knowledgeable; one who is cool in spirit has understanding. Even fools who keep silent are considered wise; when they close their lips, they are deemed intelligent.

Proverbs 17:27–28

I've figured out Americans' greatest fear: It's silence. They tolerate noise well, and they can hear voices all around them. But they can't handle silence.

One way I've shown this is to ask, "When you come home from work or an evening out, what's the first thing you do once you're inside with the lights on?" Almost invariably people tell me they turn on the TV or the radio, or they play music.

The fear of silence reminds me that the most difficult course I ever took in my final year of seminary was something called Pastoral Care 301. The seminary set up the course as an experiment—and they didn't repeat the course the following year. They broke our class of twenty-eight into four equal-sized groups.

We met twice a week for ten weeks. During the ten-week quarter, the professor never spoke one word. We had no agenda, no handouts, and no guidance. I objected because I felt there needed to be some guidelines. One student became extremely angry. Charles tried to organize us to set up our own agenda, but he never got full cooperation.

I can't speak for the others, but I became aware of something about the middle of the first class. Silence intimidated us. Each class period, I observed the anxiety painted on faces. Everyone seemed to realize that eventually someone would speak, but they waited. In one session, I had surreptitiously checked my watch as soon as the bell rang to see how long it would be before someone spoke. The silence lasted all of six minutes.

131

This says a great deal not only about our class, but about our culture as well. Maybe it says we don't want to have to face ourselves—especially in the company of other people.

Read these two verses again: "One who spares words is knowledgeable; one who is cool in spirit has understanding. Even fools who keep silent are considered wise; when they close their lips, they are deemed intelligent" (Proverbs 17:27–28).

These sayings urge us to control our talk, and they condemn excessive words. The second phrase of verse 28 was probably meant with humor, as if to say, "The fool who shuts up is no longer a complete fool."

I don't mean to commend taciturn individuals who speak only with yes or no answers. My purpose is to urge us to guard our words—especially when our speaking up can harm another person. This seems especially important when we're provoked.

Someone said to me that the best relationship is when two friends can sit beside each other and feel no need to talk. Simply being with a person you care about—and who cares about you—may be enough to erase the need for words. Mutual presence is enough.

Too often, once some people begin to speak, words gush out. "The tongue of the wise dispenses knowledge, but the mouths of fools pour out folly" (Proverbs 15:2). The endless flow of words betrays the worthlessness of their thoughts or reveals parts of their characters they don't want known. Such people often let others know how they view themselves. At best, they talk too much, and too often they talk without thinking or listening.

I understand such exhortations against speaking too much because they fit me. I'm one of those individuals who thinks fast, speaks up quickly, and talks rapidly. To people like me, these verses sound painfully important.

Proverbs emphasizes that fools speak up even though they have nothing to say in an intelligent discussion. Once they open their mouths, their foolishness becomes evident. Even so, that still doesn't stop them from speaking.

I often wonder if they *must* speak to prevent silence from

prevailing. I wonder if they'd rather be thought of as foolish or empty-headed than allow silence to intimidate them. By generating noise, at least they have some control over their situation.

A few years ago I learned a valuable lesson about silence. I was sitting with six professional writers, none of whom I had met before. One man kept the conversation filled with stories and laughs. At first, he was quite funny, but I began to grow a bit tired of his prattle. It was as if he had been hired to perform for all of us and we remained the spectators.

Finally one of the others who knew the speaker asked, "Why are you talking so much?"

Once he recovered from the shock, the loquacious person said, "I'm not comfortable with strangers and I'm always afraid that you'll talk about things I'm ignorant of. If I control the conversation, I can keep it in safe territory."

Very insightful comment. Most of us aren't that aware—and it gave me insight about myself. As I listened to that exchange, I realized that too often I've been like the talkative one. I've feared silence. And one reason is that if I allow silence to prevail, the other person may control the direction of the conversation—then I'd be really uncomfortable.

By contrast, I have one experience to share when I had lunch with four businessmen. Two of them I had known, and the other two were strangers. They spoke about issues that, although interesting to listen to, weren't matters on which I felt qualified to comment. I smiled and nodded from time to time to show I was listening—which I was. During the entire lunch period, I'm sure I never said more than six sentences.

A few days later, one of the businessmen called and invited me to lunch. Before I could express surprise and ask why he had called, he said, "You're a great conversationalist. It's nice to be around people who don't have to keep the spotlight on themselves." It's also interesting that he was the one who spoke most during lunch!

The real test for those of us who suffer from verbal diarrhea may be for us to learn to focus on others and to listen to what they say. Not only do we face the prospect of learning, it may even give the impression that we're more knowledgeable than we think we are.

Modern Proverb: *Silence can be powerful, especially when we can listen and not have to talk. Even stupid people can appear intelligent if they listen.*

Call Them Scoffers

The proud, haughty person, named "Scoffer," acts with arrogant pride.

Proverbs 21:24

I don't know whatever happened to Bertram, and it's been years since I've heard from him. He was one of the brightest individuals I'd ever met, and that's what attracted me. There wasn't any subject he didn't know about, and not many people tried to match wits with him.

Then I became a believer and that made me the butt of his insults and snide remarks. One time he said, "My role in life is to persecute you Christians to strengthen you or to make you smart enough to give it up."

For a few weeks, I actually avoided him because his words hurt. Until my conversion he had been—or so I thought—a good friend. Of all the people I had worked with, I enjoyed being with Bert more than anyone else. Now I had become his enemy and the object of his scorn.

That behavior went on for maybe five months. At first, I had joked back, but that only increased his scoffing. Mostly I said nothing. I was too new in the faith to know how to defend what I believed. I knew only that I had been miserable and that Jesus Christ had brought me peace. I told him something like that once.

"A couple of good shots of whiskey can do the same thing," he said and walked away.

I remember the last conversation we had before he transferred to a different department. We were alone in the office—both of us had gotten there before anyone else arrived. He started in on me again, and I let it go on for maybe five minutes.

"Why do you hate me so much?" I finally asked. "I've

wanted to be your friend, yet all you do is insult me and scoff at my faith."

"Maybe you have something I'll never have," he said and walked out of the office. He didn't return until the others had come. We never talked again.

I wondered about his scoffing then and through the years. Once I understood the reason for the harsh things Bert said, it helped me cope better with others like him. Maybe the loud putdowns, insults, and wisecracks are their way of saying, "I wish I could believe. I wish I had the spiritual foundation you have." Because they can't say such things, they cover it up with supposedly lighthearted words.

I'm sure it's more complex than that, but it helped me to be a little kinder and softer with such scoffers.

The verse reads: "The proud, haughty person, named 'Scoffer,' acts with arrogant pride." It contains three key words to define the scoffer: proud, haughty, and arrogant. The proverb refers to those who set themselves up as their own authority against God.

This description makes me think of Pharaoh's response when Moses asked him to let the people leave Egypt. "Who is the LORD, that I should heed him and let Israel go? I do not know the LORD, and I will not let Israel go" (Exodus 5:2).

Or another example is that of Sennacherib. During Hezekiah's reign in Judah, the Assyrian armies invaded, and King Sennacherib surrounded Jerusalem and urged the people to surrender. "Who among all the gods of the countries have delivered their countries out of my hand, that the LORD should deliver Jerusalem out of my hand?" (2 Kings 18:35).

The powerful Assyrians scoffed as they prepared to destroy one city, but in their pride, they hadn't reckoned with the intervention of Yahweh. Hezekiah and the people prayed. They received a promise of deliverance. Then we read a cryptic statement that probably meant some kind of fast-acting, deadly virus: "That very night the angel of the LORD set out and struck down one hundred eighty-five thousand in the camp of the Assyrians; when morning dawned, they were all dead bodies" (2 Kings 19:35).

As this verse makes clear, scoffers are the worst kind of fools mentioned in Proverbs. They pulsate with pride and arrogance, and they're bloated with conceit. At their best, scoffers don't respect others' point of view. They are right and have to be proven right, which means those who disagree must be wrong. At their worst, they walk around with a supercilious sneer that speaks contempt and scorn for others and for the things they hold to be of value. They're excessively arrogant and offensive. The cognate words translated *proud* and *pride* involve an exaggerated sense of self-importance expressed by being presumptuous, defiant, insolent, and rebellious.

The vanity of scoffers becomes the measure of all things and is fed by putting others down. They don't have positive words to speak about others, are quick to make cynical or harsh remarks, and are adept at throwing out objections to anyone else's plans. Such scoffers seem to delight in debunking the religious faith and moral values they have rejected.

Despite all this, there seems to me to be something else to say about scoffers—it's easier to demonstrate such an attitude than to face themselves and to face God. Some people prefer to remain ignorant rather than discover and live in the truth. They'd rather belittle than investigate possibilities. Maybe that's why the Bible speaks so disparagingly of them. They're not only closed books, but they're bound and sealed tight as well.

It reminds me of a man named Edgar with whom I did a lot of community work when I was a pastor. One day he said, "I love you, but I despise your theology and your god."

"But what if what I believe is right? Ever think about that?"

Edgar then held up his hand to stop the conversation. "I don't want to hear any more," he said.

That story illustrates how difficult it may be for some people to admit they have needs they can't provide for themselves. It's easier to scoff at those who believe.

I've been there myself. As I was writing about Edgar, it reminded me of my teen years. I crossed God and the church off my list and avoided those who spoke about either. My friends had no time for God and that was fine.

When I was in my junior year of high school, one friend

named Gene asked me to go to church with him. "Are you kidding? Do I look stupid to you? Why would I want to do something like that?"

I don't remember his immediate answer, but after we talked about it a little more, he asked, "Aren't you even willing to give God a chance?"

"Nope, I'd rather have fun," I said. After that, I made sure we never talked about God again. It would take another five years before I willingly gave God a chance—and then only because I faced the reality that I couldn't solve my own problems. I needed help—which wasn't easy to admit.

For some of us, admitting our needs and our inability to solve all our problems is a difficult transition to go through. If we stay at it, we put away our pride and arrogance. We stop scorning those whom we called weak or stupid.

I still encounter the scoffers. They have built up a system in which the human mind or science or psychology is supreme. But I wonder about something. Can they handle the consequences of what it would be like if they're wrong?

Modern Proverb: *We call them scoffers, because they'd rather sound superior than learn the truth.*

Those Terrible Addicts!

Wine is a mocker, strong drink a brawler, and whoever is led astray by it is not wise.

Proverbs 20:1

Dan and Joyce, both members of our congregation, sat across from me at a church night supper. Both of them, already fitting the label of obese, had plates filled with food about five inches high when they sat down. Frankly, I couldn't stand to watch the way Dan attacked the contents of his plate—and *attack* is the way it looked to me, much like the way an animal wolfs down food.

Even worse was the conversation. Someone mentioned people at another church who drank wine with their meals. The couple, both strict teetotalers, were aghast at such behavior. "How can they do that?" Joyce asked. "The Bible speaks against strong drink."

"Anything that harms our bodies," Dan said, "is something we need to run from."

I listened in shock as I watched their food disappear rapidly. Between large bites of potato salad and fried chicken, Dan railed on about alcohol addiction and the way it takes control of imbibers.

Then Joyce said that the closest thing to alcohol addiction was smoking.

Dan agreed, and between gulping down their ice tea and their three pieces of pie, they talked about the resulting bad health and the horrible medical costs the public had to help pay for.

I, the coward, didn't say anything, but I kept thinking, *How can you eat like that and not understand? You're both addicted and you just don't get the message, do you? Food is always on your mind and seems to be the major theme of your lives.*

I also remembered that only a couple of weeks earlier, the matter of their health had come up in a conversation—Dan's heart problems and high blood pressure, which he controlled through medication, and Joyce's diabetes that she couldn't keep under control. Both had high cholesterol levels.

As far as I was concerned, Dan and Joyce were addicts—a different kind than we find in the Bible—but addicted just as much as if they both downed a quart of Scotch every night.

Proverbs speaks against drunkenness and the way it affects people. If the sages were writing today, I suspect they would have expanded this to include anything that controls our thoughts or dictates our behavior.

An addiction, by definition, is anything that controls our lives and becomes our primary focus. And it's not easy for people to walk away from alcohol, drugs, smoking, or other powerful desires. They can't just quit. In fact, we now realize true addiction leaves the person without choice. They *must* have their fix—whatever the fix is.

Here's the best way for me to understand addiction. People hurt and they don't want to feel the pain of loneliness or rejection, so they medicate themselves. For some, drugs work. Alcohol, cocaine, sexual activity, or something like wild, uncontrolled spending—something artificial—takes away the pain.

Behind the addiction lives a hurting individual. That realization can make us more compassionate and understanding—but we don't have to tolerate those who are imprisoned by a substance or a form of behavior.

Proverbs 20:1 names two types of alcohol: wine and strong drink—the latter term probably meant beer or whiskey, which were beverages made from grapes or grain. Either could lead to intoxication and foolish behavior.

There are other temperance passages (see, for example, 23:20–21; 31:4–5; and 23:29–35). Such verses vividly develop the folly of drunkenness. And the sages not only condemned inebriation but placed drunkenness alongside laziness and adultery—because each is just as impoverishing and deadening as the others, and just as ready to seize their unwary prey.

Any mind-bending substance or bizarre behavior weakens or destroys self-control. Many substances release us from our social inhibitions and adversely affect our behavior emotionally (and even physically). In connection with this, Proverbs 23:29 asks six rhetorical questions:

1. Who has woe?
2. Who has sorrow?
3. Who has strife?
4. Who has complaining?
5. Who has wounds without cause?
6. Who has redness of eyes?

The answer appears in the last line of the verse: "Those who linger late over wine, those who keep trying mixed wines."

The common addictions seem quite limited, but the effects were just as obvious then as they are today—they result in despair, misery, quarrels, complaints, and unnecessary bruises. The proverb's reference to "red eyes" is what we'd call bloodshot eyes that become red after extended drinking or dulled from an alcoholic stupor.

And we have biblical examples for such warnings. In the book of Genesis, we have two stories of men who become drunk—Noah and Lot—both with disastrous results. (See Genesis 9:20–21; 19:30–36.)

When we think about the admonitions against drinking (and that becomes a rubric for any kind of addictive behavior), we can learn more important lessons if we think of the *principle* such proverbs speak against. The writers are concerned about giving in or surrendering to something—anything other than God.

The problem with any kind of drug is that it doesn't appeal to everyone, but can appeal to many. Dr. Joel Robertson, who has written extensively about addiction and brain chemicals, points out that most of us fit into one of two categories. Some can handle depression but not anxiety, so they take the drugs that we think of as downers, such as alcohol or marijuana. These drugs mellow them. Others are attracted to the kind that alleviate depression, and so they face temptation through the uppers. Speed (amphetamine) is an example. Those people would rather do anything than cope with feelings of sadness.

The point is that regardless of the type of personality we are, probably any of us could become hooked on some substance under the right circumstances. So the sages would say, "Run from anything that could enslave you."

Part of the warning comes because getting into drugs is easier than getting out. When I was fifteen, I began to smoke and did so until I was twenty-one. Even once I knew its bad effects—the smoker's cough, the foul odor, and most of all for me that constant desire for another smoke—it took me six months of trying a variety of methods before I finally quit cold.

That ubiquitous cigarette controlled my life. In school, I was constantly figuring out how to find an opportunity to smoke without getting caught. I spent a lot of my mental energy on that goal.

My first thought in the morning and my last at night was how to get a few puffs. Throughout the day, I constantly wanted a cigarette. Whenever I encountered stress, a cigarette calmed me.

Yet, regardless of the type of substance, whenever anything controls our thoughts, it is addictive. The best way to prove to ourselves that we're addicted is when we decide to quit! Then we realize the control such substances or behaviors have over us.

These verses in Proverbs come out of the context of a simpler, more primitive society. They saw the havoc associated with alcohol. It ruins lives—not only do the addicted suffer, but the loved ones of the addict are affected as well.

Modern Proverb: *Wisdom means not getting hooked on anything that takes us away from God.*

Wanting More

The greedy person stirs up strife, but whoever trusts in the LORD will be enriched.

Proverbs 28:25

"Greed is good," said a major character in the film *Wall Street.* Somehow that was supposed to make greed acceptable, because the man embraced the idea of grasping for it all. In fact, we live in a culture with that idea of "having it all." Such advocates don't ever seem to define "it" but stress ambition, avarice, covetousness—anything that will propel people to go all the way to get more and to win "it" all.

They also never tell us what to do with it when we've got it all. In fact, for those with such a philosophy there never is an end. They always want more.

Isn't it interesting that only one of the Ten Commandments refers to attitude rather than action? It's the last one (Exodus 20:17), which says we're not to covet. The problem is that if the attitude is one of getting, accumulating, desiring, and wanting more, action will follow.

For the sages, greed wasn't a private vice; it was a public issue. They said (as in the proverb) that greed stirred up strife. The same word, translated *envy* in verse 3:31, may mean an intense desire that motivates people to act. It may be thought of positively as the call that inspires us to work hard, long, and effectively to achieve legitimate goals or to support a worthy cause. Too often, however, it's a strong desire for another's quality, condition, or property that prompts us to use sinful or questionable means to get what we want.

When I say that greed stirs up strife, one of the places that it stirs is *within.* The covetous grasp and scheme to get as much as they can have—as well as yearn for the things they can't ever have. Despite all their schemes, they're never content—which is the way greed works.

James pointedly asks in verses 4:1–2: "Those conflicts and disputes among you, where do they come from? Do they not come from your cravings that are at war within you?" Strange, isn't it, that James is writing to *believers?* He's saying that the very ones we would expect to have life figured out—and to be content with their lot in life—are as greedy as people outside the faith.

When we stop to think about it, there are few quarrels or wars where greed isn't somewhere at or near the root—whether it's greed for money, power, position, or prestige.

I wonder if greed doesn't come from internal emptiness. When we don't have a healthy sense of who we are or know that we're loved and valuable just because of who we are, then we turn our desires outward. We seek to accumulate things to take our minds off our need for love and acceptance.

Maybe we'll never fully destroy greed in our lives, but it's certainly one thing that troubles us constantly. We live in a sales-driven world where we buy products that are built for obsolescence. Olive gray was last year's car color, and teal blue is this year's fashion tone. If we're wearing rust, we're at least two years out of date. One year the kids demand Reebok sneakers, but the next year a new brand beckons. That's how it works. Until perhaps sixty years ago, we bought products to last. Our dining room furniture lasted a lifetime, and we passed on our dishes to the next generation.

Is it possible that with all the growing affluence in this country, we're also breeding an emptier, more isolated generation? Could it be that instead of rejoicing in what we have, we think we'll find fulfillment only with having more? Instead of looking inwardly—that is, to God—do we seek to find our salvation through outward acquisition?

I once asked a wealthy man if he was happy. He had just finished showing me a magnificent mansion he had just moved into.

"Am I happy? I have this house, don't I?" he said and moved on to another topic. Displaying his beautiful property was supposed to shout yes at me.

Instead, his answer saddened me.

I'm sure he didn't know the exhortation the older Paul wrote to the younger Timothy that there is great gain in godliness with contentment. (See 1 Timothy 6:6.)

Maybe it helps if we examine ourselves and ask if we're trying to hide our spiritual impoverishment by outward adornment. Our churches are larger and more ornate, and I wonder if beautiful architecture is supposed to replace spirituality. Instead of beat-up Fords and rusted Chevys, the church parking lots are filled with SUVs, Lexus sedans, and a variety of vans. We justify our needs for them and once we have them, we ask how we ever survived without such things.

I'm not opposed to having things or enjoying our lifestyle, but maybe we need to go back to the Tenth Commandment. Maybe we need to start with motives instead of looking at results. I know that as long as we give in to the raging need for more, bigger, newer, or shinier, we'll have internal strife, even if we silence the outward noises. Inner peace—the kind that Jesus Christ gives and the only kind that lasts—is to examine those motives, to open them up to God.

At the Last Supper, Jesus said one of those at the table with him would betray him. Maybe we need to think of that when it comes to greed. Maybe we need to respond as each of the disciples did: "Lord, is it I?"

Good question.

Is it I, Lord? Is it I?

Modern Proverb: *When we don't put our trust in God, we put it in the outward life—and greed is the power that drives us. Wanting and yearning to acquire more fills us with internal strife. Peace is being thankful for what God gives us.*

Giving Means Getting

Some give freely, yet grow all the richer; others withhold what is due, and only suffer want.

Proverbs 11:24

I heard a story about hoarding during World War II. The government rationed sugar, nylon, tires, and other rubber products—anything that it needed for the war effort. No company made automobiles for consumers because they all went to the military.

Once the federal government announced the rationing, a number of people began hoarding. Apparently one family filled most of their basement closet with one- and five-pound packages of sugar, and an immense amount of anything rationed. They had bought a supply of automobile tires and a large number of boxes of canned meats.

They had a teenage son who was active in church, and he realized what a selfish thing his parents had done. Secretly, he began to give the rationed goods to needy families in the neighborhood. "Please, don't say anything to anyone," the boy would say. "You know where the Bible says not to let the left hand know what the right hand is doing." Apparently, his parents never discovered what he had done.

The war ended, and the following spring, their city faced torrential rains. The hoarding family's waterfront property flooded—including the basement closet that contained the sugar—and then rose to the main floor. Every bag in the basement had been not only soaked, but broken. The canned goods had rusted. The family's hoarding had come to nothing. They suffered the most severe loss of any other family in the community. They couldn't cook food or bathe for almost two weeks and had no electricity for several days.

As soon as the word of that family's need spread, neighbors brought in cooked meals and gave them free access to their bathrooms. The parents were awed by the generosity.

"You did so much for us," one of the neighbors said, "by sending over all those things when we needed them."

After several families gave them the mysterious message, the son finally confessed what he had done. His giving had resulted in blessings.

And maybe that's a good parable about life—the more we give, the more we receive.

Several proverbs teach the important principle of generosity, and it's stated quite simply: Those who give will receive even more than they give to others. When explaining this principle in agricultural terms for the people of the Old Testament, the sages spoke of being refreshed by water (literally "rain")— an absolute necessity for their way of life.

By contrast, the stingy withhold what they should give, and in the long run, they end up being the losers. Paul wrote the principle to the Corinthian church this way: "The point is this: the one who sows sparingly will also reap sparingly, and the one who sows bountifully will also reap bountifully" (2 Corinthians 9:6).

Paul didn't write mere theory about giving, but he referred to a real situation that existed. Acts 11 records that a prophet named Agabus prophesied a serious famine would descend on the land of Israel. Paul and Barnabas went out among the newly formed churches, asking them to give generously to those in Israel. In Second Corinthians, Paul points out that they had been among the first churches to promise aid, and he had boasted about their example to the others. Now he was sending brothers to collect the generous gift they had promised. He adds, "Each of you must give as you have made up your mind, not reluctantly or under compulsion, for God loves a cheerful giver" (2 Corinthians 9:7). He assures them that God will provide abundantly for them if they give generous alms to those in need.

The remarkable principle works—except when we give in order to get. Nowhere is this better illustrated than in the book of Acts. In the early days of the church, Christians lived in some kind of communal setting before persecution drove them out of Jerusalem.

Luke speaks about believers selling property and giving so that they were of one heart. "There was not a needy person among them" (Acts 4:34). In the midst of that situation, a Levite named Joseph sold a field and gave the money to the apostles. Apparently, in appreciation for his generosity, they changed the man's name to Barnabas, which means "son of encouragement" (see 4:36).

The text goes on to recount the story of Ananias and his wife Sapphira, who sold property, held back part of the money, and brought the rest to Peter, claiming they had given the entire amount.

Although the Bible doesn't say this, because it immediately follows the story of Barnabas's generosity, I think it's a way to say that the couple wanted the praise and thanks he received, so they tried to imitate him—well, partially. They wanted to give part and have others believe they had given all.

Peter faced them and said that when the property belonged to them, they didn't have to sell it, and even after they sold it, the money was still theirs. They had lied and deceived by pretending to give more than they did. "How is it that you have contrived this deed in your heart? You did not lie to us but to God!" (Acts 5:4). Both of them were struck dead!

As I've understood giving in the Bible, the principles are simple. God expects a tenth (a tithe), a custom in vogue long before the Law of Moses and hundreds of years before Jesus Christ. That's like a debt or a payment for being alive on the earth. Beyond that, we give offerings.

The amount we give depends on our own heart. God loves (that is, blesses) those who give generously—whether in material things or in spiritual benefits—and they come out ahead. What we get depends largely on what we give. If we open ourselves to God, we receive the blessings of God freely.

Modern Proverb: *If we want true wealth, we get it by giving to others in need. God loves it when we give generously, and God shows that pleasure by blessing our lives.*

Generous Souls

A generous person will be enriched, and one who gives
water will get water.

Proverbs 11:25

God has built an important principle in the universe, and one that too many people never understand: Givers receive even more than they give. Jesus stated the principle this way: "Give, and it will be given to you. A good measure, pressed down, shaken together, running over, will be put into your lap; for the measure you give will be the measure you get back" (Luke 6:38).

In the proverb, the "one who gives water" literally means the "one who rains" blessings on others. Ancients would have grasped that idea easily. Refreshing water—the rain—revitalized the land in that dry climate, and their lives revolved around the amount of moisture they received each rainy season. So the sages say, in effect: "Those who rain abundantly and generously upon others will themselves be well provided for." It's not meant as an inducement to give, like a mechanical law, so that anytime we give, we're assured of getting at least an equal amount in return. If we give just to receive in return, maybe we're missing the inherent principle.

This proverb doesn't spell out *what* the generous receive, but certainly such people end up better off—perhaps not always financially or materially, but certainly happier. Those who attach more importance to meeting human needs than to maximizing profits earn a good reputation and approval expressed in the blessing.

This generous giving became clear to me when PBS showed a film from the 1990s that affected many viewers. Even though

I had seen it in the theater and knew what was coming, in the last scene, tears flooded my eyes as spontaneously as they did the first time.

Mr. Holland's Opus centers on a talented musician, played by Richard Dreyfuss, who becomes a high school band instructor to support himself—temporarily. His goal is to write his own music, but it just doesn't work out. He never quite finds the energy to finish his opus because he gives himself so thoroughly to his students. He thinks he'll compose his music during the summer, but instead, he works with students. The years roll along, and Mr. Holland stays at the high school, teaching and giving generously of himself.

At the end of the film, Holland is forced to retire. Without his knowledge, many of his former students return, and in a surprising finale, they play the opus that Mr. Holland had worked on for years (the music obviously supplied by Holland's wife) and they play *for him.* It's a poignant and powerful moment in the film.

No one says so in words, but it's obvious that Mr. Holland's opus wasn't the music he composed. His greatest "music" was the students to whom he gave himself, and that "music" lived on through their lives.

That's how generosity works. It's not a matter of donating $100 so that God will return an equal amount, or $200, or $1,000. It means we give because it's the right thing to do, because the needs are there, or sometimes because, as this proverb says, it's "what is due."

For most of us today when it comes to money, the due that seems the most obvious is the giving of the ancient tithe (or tenth) of our income.

In a meeting of ministers, one man argued against tithing because "it's Old Testament law."

Before I could open my mouth, my pastor-friend Oliver Wood said, "Then I assume you believe in the superiority of grace." The man nodded. "That being so, I also assume you want to give more than ten percent!" (Oliver went on to point out that the biblical principle was established in the story of Abraham giving a tithe to King Melchizedek in Genesis 14:17–20.)

Regardless, whether it's a matter of law or obligation or grace, doesn't giving one-tenth as thanks to God seem so little anyway? Years ago I heard a preacher say, "Let your giving be according to your income, lest God make your income according to your giving."

Let's think a little more about giving. First, generosity is a way of saying thanks to God, a way of acknowledging the goodness of God.

Second, giving also says something else—it says, "I'm making this an act of faith." Too many people have said, "I'd like to give more to God, but I just can't afford it."

The true giving that God loves comes from the heart that says, "I trust God. If I give at least one-tenth, God can do a miracle equal to the five loaves and two fish to feed five thousand. That is, God can stretch the remaining amount to provide abundantly for every need I have."

I want to illustrate the principle of giving by which I have lived since I was twenty-two years old. Within a few months after I had been converted from agnosticism to the Christian faith, I heard a sermon that changed my life. The widow of the founder of an international corporation spoke at our church about the principle of the tithe. When she and her husband first went into business, they felt God wanted them to take ten percent of the gross profit and give it to God—even before they accounted for their expenses. She spoke a lot more and quoted Bible verses, but the impact of that message hit me through one of those verses. She read from Malachi 3, where God accuses the Jews of robbing him by not paying their tithes. When she read, I felt as if God pounded my chest with a huge fist: "Bring ye all the tithes into the storehouse . . . and prove me now herewith, saith the LORD of hosts, if I will not open you the windows of heaven, and pour you out a blessing that there shall not be room enough to receive it" (Malachi 3:10 KJV).

At the time, I was single and in the U.S. Navy. I had been transferred from the East Coast to Great Lakes, Illinois, and in the process, my pay records had been lost. I received something like $30 a month. (It took them nearly six months to find my papers because someone had misspelled my last name.)

When I heard that message about giving ten percent, I thought, *I can't do that. I'm barely surviving now.* But the impact didn't go away. For days I thought about the woman's words and especially the quotation from Malachi. I argued with myself, explained and complained to God, but I had no peace.

For at least two weeks, I prayed and struggled over the matter. Then one morning when I was standing in the chow line, I realized something. The matter of the $3 a month wasn't the real issue. I was having a struggle of faith. Could I trust God to provide for my needs? If I made God's business my business, would God make my business divine business?

Then I got angry. "Okay, God, if you won't give me any peace, I'll put you to the test! Malachi promises that you'll provide for me if I give you 10 percent of my income. Okay, I'm going to give you *15 percent*! Now let's see what you'll do." The following Sunday I gave 15 percent.

I can only say that through all the years since then, I've never missed a meal or lacked any material thing I've needed. Most of all, I've learned to give of my money, my time, and my gifts to others. I feel I get the best deal out of it. I receive so much more than I give.

I like to think of it this way: Those who generously rain upon others will be refreshed from the abundance of showers. Here's the way I express my understanding of giving: God shovels it in, I shovel it out, and God has the larger shovel.

Modern Proverb: *Those who generously rain blessings upon others will themselves be refreshed by an abundance of showers.*

Richer or Poorer

The rich and the poor have this in common: the LORD is
the maker of them all.

Proverbs 22:2

"God ordained some to be poor and others to have money," the
man argued. "If we give to the poor, we disrupt God's plan."
He quoted this verse and the words of Jesus: "The poor you
will always have with you."

He carefully avoided mentioning verses about giving to the
poor or the needy. I think I understood. He didn't want to share
his money with anyone, and being an active church member,
he had to justify to himself and perhaps to others that he was
doing the right thing by not giving to "those worthless people"
who wouldn't do anything for themselves.

Yes, it's true we'll always have at least two distinct classes
of people. This proverb isn't advocating it, only stating the
obvious. Within the world that God created and controls, the
rich and the poor, as well as the oppressors of the poor, are
there side by side. Yet they're not saying that this state of
affairs lies with God and merits the divine seal of approval.

However, the reality stands before us every day. Some people are rich and others aren't. It's a fact. Some can afford the
two-million-dollar homes and drive cars that cost $100,000,
while in the same city are those who rent tiny apartments, live
in homeless shelters, and ride the bus.

The sages didn't try to work out a political theory or set up
a theological framework; they weren't reformers, but observers.
Although they didn't say it, the implication is that the rich and
the poor approach each other at many times in life. They meet
in birth because there's no other way into this life—everyone

enters naked, helpless, and barely conscious into the world. All stand as sinners before a loving God. Throughout life, all are subject to the same sorrows, sicknesses, infirmities, and temptations. Finally, they meet again in the grave—dust to dust—and their money won't buy them out of that experience. Ultimately, the Bible teaches, the rich and the poor stand side by side at the final judgment to give account to God of their lives—and there are no special seats for the privileged!

God creates us all, and we're all objects of God's love. Because God cares, it follows that we were created to care for others, regardless of their social or financial status.

I was thinking of a friend named Harriette who volunteered to deliver food for a group called Meals on Wheels. One day she was to take food to one of the most beautiful mansions she had ever seen. As she drove up the long driveway, she felt herself seething with resentment. *Look at the money these people must have,* she thought, *and now they take charity!*

At the door, an elderly woman, crippled with arthritis, invited her inside. She wore a beautiful and obviously expensive dress. A fresh wave of anger flowed through Harriette. "I wanted to throw the food in her face," she told a group of us later.

"You're extremely kind to do this," the woman said. "I know it's such a long drive for you, and I appreciate this more than you know."

That attitude surprised Harriette and caught her off guard.

"My husband left me," she said. "I have a big house, but I can't get the deed to sell. I still have all these beautiful clothes, but I don't even have enough money to buy food. If you people didn't bring me these meals, I don't know what I'd do."

That formerly rich woman's poverty taught Harriette a great deal, and it helped her realize that she was to reach out to those in need and not on the basis of whether they had money or didn't, or the way she perceived their status in life.

What Harriette learned, and the lesson many of us need, is that God cares for everyone. There's no income line where divine love stops.

As I thought of this, it makes me wonder if God is trying to say to us that personal worth is more important than personal wealth.

God doesn't measure value by the figures in a bank account.

If that's true, what would it be like if we accepted people for who they are inside and ignore what they wear or drive, or where they live? What would it be like if we accepted one another first as human beings?

In our culture today, aside from the very rich and the extremely poor, most of us fit into that general group called middle class. Wealth may not tempt us as much as in former times. If they were writing today, perhaps the sages would contrast the famous and the ordinary. There's something about being famous in our culture that puts celebrities on a level that's just a bit higher than ordinary people. For example, it's incredible to me that a woman could be a living ad for a diet center simply because of her sexual improprieties with a president. We've elevated her to celebrity status for such reprehensible behavior.

The famous and the notorious do get treated differently. Years ago when I wrote the biography of the singer B. J. Thomas, he spoke of having been a drug addict and getting away with it: "When you're a big name, people let you get away with a lot."

Entertainers, politicians, and sports figures—they've taken the place of the powerfully rich (although some of them may be wealthy as well). Maybe it's enough to repeat, "God loves them as much as God loves us."

I've met a number of famous personalities and ghostwritten their autobiographies, and I realized that I'm as happy as they are. In fact, I'm a lot happier than most of them.

They're lionized and followed around, and people yearn for attention from them. The sad thing is that those celebrities aren't that different from us. They yearn for love, acceptance, and peace—just as all the rest of us. Actor Peter Falk once said, "Don't confuse success with happiness."

Too often those high-profiled individuals have to settle for adulation or cult status, and feel they can't be real people.

Maybe those people need our pity as much as our prayers.

Modern Proverb: *Whether rich or poor, famous or ordinary, God loves us all—and wants us to love, too.*

Delayed Results

*Hope deferred makes the heart sick, but a desire fulfilled
is a tree of life.*

Proverbs 13:12

The other day I wondered about Jesus' disciples between the
betrayal by Judas and the resurrection. What were their thoughts
about all the events of those crucial days? How did they handle
the loss of Jesus, their long-awaited Messiah who died? Did
Jesus' death destroy all their expectations? Did they still maintain a flicker of hope?

We don't know what they did, how they felt, or what they
thought. Maybe they sat around and mourned, frequently
checking to make sure that the Roman soldiers or Temple offi-
cials weren't searching for them. What a low period that must
have been for that group of men.

I wonder if Peter said something like "We hoped, because
we were certain Jesus was the one, but we were wrong." They
were left with saddened hearts and spoiled dreams.

The only story we have in the New Testament that gives us
any clue is found in Luke's Gospel. It's the story of two other
followers who walked from Jerusalem to Emmaus, a trip of
about seven miles. (See Luke 24:13–35.) Along the way, Jesus
joined them. In such cultures, for a stranger to join people
going the same direction wouldn't have been unusual. People
often walked together just to have company as they traveled
the long distances. Although we don't know the reason, they
didn't recognize Jesus.

Jesus asked what they were talking about. An amazed
Cleopas asked Jesus if he was the only person around Jerusalem
who didn't know what was going on. Cleopas told the stranger

about the mighty prophet in whom they placed their hopes, and the Romans had crucified him: "But we had hoped that he was the one to redeem Israel" (Luke 24:21).

What sad, disillusioned men. They had hoped—and when the Bible uses *hope,* it's not wishing or desiring, but the sense of expectation. Cleopas might just as well have said, "We believed in him and now he's dead and all our faith has died with him."

Modern expectations probably haven't been quite that high or our disappointments quite that severe, but all of us know the sadness of expecting something positive to happen, only to have it fail to materialize.

For instance, I remember at the end of my first year in graduate school, a group of us hurried to a bulletin board as soon as we learned that they had posted grades for a particular course. They listed us by social security number so that our names didn't appear. The grade in one course in particular depended on a final project; a number of students had been nervous about it. I had expected to do well and I did.

As I turned to walk away, I saw Ron standing there, saying nothing to anyone. I didn't have to ask his grade, because his face said it all. Only the day before, he had talked about his project, obviously believing it would be one of the best in the class. He was just as obviously wrong.

Ron felt so dejected by that grade, he dropped out of school. I ran into him months later and he complained about the "lousy grading system, the unfair professors, and the intense pressures put on students." His bitterness saddened me. Maybe that's what the proverb means by "hope deferred makes the heart sick." In Ron's case, the sickness was his angry and still-hurt attitude.

As the proverb states, when we expect something and don't get it, it casts us down—perhaps even into depression. It also goes on to point out the joy of getting what we yearn for.

The unknown sages who wrote this proverb must have observed many different situations where people waited and hoped. For many of them, those hopes were based on prayers, on crying out to God, or maybe on their commitment to trust God's mercy.

What happened when those expectations didn't find fulfillment? We can easily imagine the people saying:

- "We believed that the Messiah had come and now he's dead and in the tomb."
- "We were sure we'd always have a king on the throne in Jerusalem, but the city is nothing but ruins."
- "We expected God to deliver us from the Babylonians, but here we are in exile."
- "We were certain that the Temple would stand and that no enemies would ever destroy it."

When the Jews returned from exile, I assume they had many dreams that sprang from anticipation. I wonder how many of them expected they'd go back to Jerusalem and life would be filled with God's protection? If so, they had sad experiences to face. They had to rebuild everything, and all the while, their enemies schemed to destroy them. At one time, conditions deteriorated so that half the people worked while the other half stood guard.

We don't have to confine expectations to the Old Testament or even to the Bible to see such dashed hopes. We've all had those deep longings, those hopes that kept us going and that have propelled us forward. Then our dreams vanish.

When I was a teenager, I remember a man named Irwin Shell, who moved away from his parents' home in northern Minnesota and took a low-paying job in the city where I lived in Iowa. He had one dream—to be a writer. He rarely talked about anything else.

I worked after school at the same place, and Irwin must have told me the plot of his novel eight times. It seemed like a good story to me.

When he wasn't working, Irwin was pecking away on his typewriter, writing and rewriting his novel. Over the year or so, every publisher and agent he contacted turned it down. In the middle of his second winter, Irwin stopped writing and became seriously ill. One day, the owner of our workplace called to say that he had taken Irwin to the hospital. The next day, Irwin died of pneumonia.

I wonder if pneumonia is what really killed him. Did he give up because his dreams and desires had vanished? Is it possible that when he had nothing to live for, he stopped living? As I think of Irwin, I wonder if it isn't better to cling to high hopes without seeing their realization than it is to be content with low hopes that are easily satisfied.

Hope deferred is certainly better than hope destroyed, as in Irwin's case. But the nature of expectation is that desire yearns for fulfillment. People will work long and hard providing they believe that their efforts will pay off in the future.

When all hopes die, so often the human spirit dies as well. With that in mind, it's easy to understand the discouragement of Jesus' disciples after the crucifixion.

Then Jesus appeared and renewed their hope. Before he left the two men on the road to Emmaus, they knew who he was and that the Messiah lived. Their expectations, which they thought had died on Friday with the crucifixion, underwent a marvelous resurrection. Now they understood the other part of that proverb: "a desire fulfilled is a tree of life" (or a life-giving tree).

One final point stems from my own experience. When I chose to leave the pastorate after fourteen years and become a full-time writer, I prepared as much as possible. Not only was I selling regularly and lining up projects, I talked to successful entrepreneurs and then read articles and books by and about them. I discovered an interesting phenomenon among many who had become successful. They started with a dream—an assurance that they were going to make it. They willingly took the risks because they were convinced they could make their dreams come true.

I especially enjoyed the parts where they wrote about the dark days. Most of them had those experiences as they were nearing the end of the road. They reached the place where they weren't sure they would survive. Although they said it differently, the various statements went something like this:

- "I reached the place where I didn't know if it was worth going on."

- "I was ready to give up and go get a job with a guaranteed salary."
- "I decided I was probably fooling myself and it was stupid to hold on."

Yet those people eventually became successful! They didn't quit, even though their candles burned low. Even when the candles barely flickered, something kept them burning. They reported that it was the holding on at the darkest point that made the difference. "Once you've been to the bottom," one successful man said, "you're not afraid of risks again. You just hang tight and you know that up is the only way to go."

As my friend ultra-marathon runner Stan Cottrell says, "I've often found that the difference between success or defeat is holding on five more minutes. When all logic screams at you to quit . . . hold on five more minutes!"

His advice is much like the attitude of those entrepreneurial winners. Once they had passed through the deepest, darkest valley of despair and yet still held on, their companies became successful. Maybe that has to happen to many of us as it did to the disciples on the way to Emmaus. Maybe we have to reach the place of despair before we can truly value the joy of having that dream fulfilled.

Modern Proverb: *Waiting and longing can be difficult. But if we stay with our desires, those fulfilled dreams breathe new life into us.*

Taking the Right Road

The highway of the upright avoids evil; those who guard their way preserve their lives.

Proverbs 16:17

I was still a novice at hiking and it was my second time in the winter. My traveling companion, an experienced hiker, had gone ahead to break the path for me and was about a quarter mile ahead of me, or at least far enough that I couldn't see him.

Everything was going fine despite the freezing temperatures, the crusty snow, and icy patches that sneaked up on us. The worst moment came for me when we had to cross a small river. One log, about nine inches wide, provided the only means to get to the other side. Several patches of ice hugged the middle of it. My backpack, which weighed about thirty-five pounds, was well balanced. I looked down at the stream, maybe ten feet below, lightly frozen over in spots. If I fell, I wasn't sure I could right myself and get out of the freezing water.

Frankly, I was scared. My mind filled with everything that could go wrong. I had no questions about being able to walk across, but I wasn't sure how steadily I could make it with the heavy pack. I took my first step, stopped, and stared at the freezing waters. Then I thought, *I'll get more scared if I look down.* I looked across the stream, which wasn't farther than a dozen feet, and saw a beautiful straight tree about a foot beyond the end of the log. I set my gaze on that tree and walked slowly across the log. I made it.

That experience reminds me of this proverb. If we set our goals and allow nothing to divert us or to throw us off track, we will make it. That statement can function as great encouragement to us as we hike our way through life.

And yet in some ways, it's a troubling statement. If the words mean that when we trust God, we're no longer at risk or we won't have any terrible calamities, common sense whispers, "That can't be true." But the proverb isn't making a claim that says nothing bad will ever happen to those who seek God.

"The highway of the upright avoids evil." The word translated as *avoids* means *turn aside from* and is used to represent individuals walking along the path of the righteous. They actively make choices that escape any kind of evil. The proverb wants us to realize that we need to make wise choices that guard us from many of life's corruptions and keep us on a safe path.

This proverb makes me aware of two problems. First, we don't always recognize evil for what it is. In fact, I suspect that most of the wicked deeds that good people commit are because they have found ways to justify their actions and have convinced themselves either that they're doing good or that they have no other choice.

Why not? We learned the lesson from Adam and Eve in the garden. When the serpent tempted them to eat of the forbidden fruit, the Bible records an interesting response. God had said they could eat anything they wanted, although they were to avoid the fruit of only *one* tree.

The tempter said that if they ate, their eyes would be opened and they would be like God—that is, they would know good and evil. That's not asking them to do anything bad. In fact, it suggests such an action would improve their lives.

"So when the woman saw . . . that it was a delight to the eyes, and that the tree was to be desired to make one wise, she took of its fruit and ate . . ." (Genesis 3:6).

We use the same patterns today. Instead of admitting we're walking down Destruction Boulevard, we justify our behavior. For instance, after we lose our temper and speak harshly to someone, we say, "I was standing up for myself," "She deserved it," or "He started it."

When we can find ways in our own minds to justify our wrong behavior, it suddenly turns from being evil to being the right thing to do. Here's an example of how I trapped myself not long ago. I started telling someone a true-but-unkind piece of information about a third person. As soon as I said it, a voice within nagged at me. The right thing would have been for me to apologize, but I didn't. I told myself, *I'm only speaking the truth. It's not a lie, so that makes it all right.*

Second, life isn't always so clear. How do we know when to hang left or turn right? The sages believed they lived in an orderly world in which God rewarded good conduct and punished bad—and usually quite soon after the deed. In some of their writings they link the acts and consequences as a natural order. For them, this world is a good and marvelous place for the righteous, but an extremely bad one for the wicked.

We live in a totally different time, and life no longer seems quite as simple. In our time, good people don't always prosper and sometimes the wicked don't suffer. In reading the entire book of Proverbs, however, I don't think the sages were quite as naive as it might appear. They acknowledged that the wicked sometimes prospered and the righteous often experienced misfortune, but that didn't deter them from their pronouncements. If the proverbs tell us the way an ideal world turns, we only have to read Job to grasp a grittier version of life. Yet elsewhere they write: "Do not fret because of evildoers. Do not envy the wicked; for the evil have no future; the lamp of the wicked will go out" (24:19–20).

We don't want to forget that the proverbs constantly contrast the two ways or two lifestyles that lead to ultimate destinations. They stress that the choice of direction leads to the ultimate end. Choosing the right path means turning away whenever we encounter evil opportunities or face temptations.

Avoiding evil protects the inward life from harm. But it doesn't mean that harm, evil, or bad things don't happen. Rather, the sages warn that wrong behavior produces bad results. They stress the urgency of following the straight path, no matter what happens along the way. If we keep our eyes on the end of the road and don't deviate, we'll find the blessings of God on our lives. We're to concentrate on moving directly toward our goals without allowing distractions to come in.

Modern Proverb: *If we follow God, we can't always avoid problems, but we know where we're going. If we don't deviate, we'll come out all right in the end.*

Wait a Second!

*To guarantee loans for a stranger brings trouble, but
there is safety in refusing to do so.*

Proverbs 11:15

Most of us respond to emotional appeals. We Americans have
learned to reach out to victims of hurricanes or burned-out
houses, or those with deep personal needs. Sometimes, however, we might be wiser if we held back until we were certain
it was the right thing to do.

This verse appears like a warning label on a product, urging
us to think carefully before we make commitments. This fore-
warning, also repeated in slightly different forms in 17:18 and
22:16, refers to fiscal matters.

In our modern world we have ways to check credit balances, and there are collection procedures. That's quite an evo-
lution since the days of the sages. In that era, people lived in
small villages—even the largest cities were much smaller than
anything we would call by that term today. Virtually everyone
in the area knew each other—and not only knew the others but
could tell you who their parents were and their parents before
them and back several more generations.

The stranger, then, wouldn't likely be someone who had
moved into the village and within a month asked neighbors for
loans. The "stranger" probably referred to those not directly
connected by business or blood. It's a way of saying, "Don't be
too trusting or too easily taken in by people you don't know
well."

Another factor is that the practice of "suretyship" was a
common means to get loans. The sages may specifically have
meant the complex credit arrangements made by the merchants

and traders. If that's the case, their warning words apply to anyone who considered underwriting the debts of a friend, relative, or neighbor who had fallen on hard times. We don't use words like *suretyship* today, but it was the too-easy assumption of debts or obligations of others.

The advice then says, "Signing for a loan isn't a smart thing to do, especially if you don't know the person well." Practical wisdom says that the sages must have seen many debtors default and enough well-intentioned guarantors lose money and suffer for their rash generosity.

This warning makes me think of Jeannie, who came to talk to me, absolutely devastated by harsh treatment by several people in the church.

"I just wanted to help," Jeannie said as tears glided down her cheeks. She had joined our church six months earlier and immediately plunged into a variety of activities and volunteer programs. Jeannie was always there when needed.

Maybe that was her biggest problem. She was always there, always trying to do everything. Instead of building goodwill, she built up a lot of resentment.

People like Jeannie have a zeal to make the world better, to save others, to lift others from the bottom. And that's not a bad idea. But it's important to know the motive behind the actions. Jeannie was what we sometimes call an enabler, or a co-dependent-helper type who quickly rushes out to rescue anyone in the name of Jesus Christ, love, humanity, or common decency. Jeannie's (probably unconscious) ongoing project was to find those with messed-up lives, the needy, and those living unhealthy lives.

People like Jeannie have an acute sense of responsibility to deliver others from pain, to end unhappiness, and to do whatever necessary to bring healing to the hurting. They make promises—often larger ones than they can possibly keep—and they exhaust themselves trying to be helpers. "I'll always be here for you" or "You can trust me with anything."

Yet there's something good about such helpers. They set standards that many of us would do well to take note of. True, they may be as unhealthy as those they seek to help, but they're committed to action. They don't pass by on the other side of the road when they see hurting individuals. Yet it's unfortunate that they have no boundary line. Once they've crossed into private territory, they have no idea where to stop.

The Jeannies of this world would do well to grasp the reality that no human love can heal anyone. We can reach out, care, offer help, and lift the weak, but we also have to recognize when we shouldn't help. Sometimes the most helpful thing we can do is to do nothing. Maybe those who have fallen down need to learn to depend on God, pick themselves up, or begin to walk on their own feet instead of being carried.

That's the important message behind this proverb. Although the sages wrote against guaranteeing a loan for a stranger, their words imply much more.

I offer one caution about this verse: The selfish and uncaring can grasp and quote such verses as justification for not doing anything. They can cite this as a way to weaken character or to take over others' responsibility for themselves.

Those are the people who won't give to help the needy and even quote the words of Jesus: "For you always have the poor with you" (Matthew 26:11). And, by the way, Jesus wasn't saying that was God's ordained way. He rebuked his disciples because they objected when a woman brought in expensive ointment and anointed him. They thought she should have sold it and given the money to the poor. Jesus told them to be quiet, because that woman had performed a good service. "By pouring this ointment on my body she has prepared me for burial" (v. 12).

The proverb isn't intended to dry up helpful sympathy, but it's a message against incautious kindness. It's to hold up a warning hand to the rash or the ill-considered pledges. Don't we always have the kind-hearted who see a need and rush in to fill it? They're the types who can't say no. Or as one of my friends often says, "They're the people who keep seeking a cross to climb up on." Such actions may cost the generous person dearly afterward.

Of course, there are times to help, times to reach out to the stranger. And *stranger* can be a synonym for *another* and not just people we don't know. Aren't there times when friends, neighbors, and co-workers need our help and we can come to their aid? Too often today we limit our benevolent acts to something that really isn't wisdom and probably doesn't flow with the wisdom of this proverb.

Let's keep our hearts open to hurt around us and be willing to reach out to those in need. Before we take the final step, however, let's ask, "God, is this something you want me to do? Should I say no?"

Modern Proverb: *Be sure you know what you're doing before you make serious commitments.*

Kind Rewards

Those who are kind reward themselves, but the cruel do themselves harm.

Proverbs 11:17

It takes little effort to be kind.

That's a principle I've tried to remind myself of for the past twenty years. We can state the principle in many ways. The most obvious is to love our neighbors as we love ourselves. Isn't it unfortunate that the loving-our-neighbors idea has gotten overworked and underpracticed, and too often the words mean nothing?

Most of the time, kindness takes little effort and can make a difference to others. For example, one morning I was out running before daylight. We have a tricky intersection where there's a little V-shaped wedge and traffic gets heavy by 5:30. I had to cross the busy intersection. I got to the middle to wait in the turn lane, which becomes a regular lane fifty feet farther ahead. Just then a car was trying to make a left turn out of a short street that's less than a hundred feet from the V-shape.

Here's what happened. The left-turn driver had his turn signals on, and the first oncoming car stopped and waited for the person to make his turn. The driver in the next car blew his horn, but the man in the lead car waited anyway. Then he stuck his arm out the window and waved me across. I signaled my thanks and raced across. That was a small, simple act of kindness.

The second driver in line may not have thought so, but at least two of us felt grateful. The entire incident had taken maybe four seconds. I'm not sure what the impatient second-in-line would have done with those gained seconds, but my

169

guess is that the driver who waited must have felt good for his act of thoughtfulness.

I think of the beautiful promise: "If you offer your food to the hungry and satisfy the needs of the afflicted, then your light shall rise in the darkness and your gloom be like the noonday. The LORD will guide you continually, and satisfy your needs . . ." (Isaiah 58:10–11).

Not long ago I became aware of this principle in action. Two women I had known for years were both lonely and constantly reaching out for attention. Both were members of the church where I was once the pastor. One of them, whom I'll call June, was in the hospital. The pastor was out of town and someone persuaded Ellie to visit as a representative of the church. As a result, the two women developed a warm friendship. Ellie had been widowed for two years before the hospital visit, and June's husband died within months after that hospital visit.

When I saw both women at a social function, they were smiling and cheerful. That amazed me because I'd never seen such pleasant expressions on either face before. Both were doing volunteer work at the church and in the community.

As I thought about it, I realized this delightful situation came about because Ellie had done *one* kind deed. And look at the resulting benefits both women have reaped.

Let's focus on the second half of the proverb: "the cruel do themselves harm." As I read those words, I thought of the encounter in the Bible between the prophet Elijah and King Ahab.

Before their historic face-off, Ahab had already become known as a wicked king. He and his wife Jezebel perverted the way of Yahweh at every turn, including the elevation of pagan worship. Elijah then declared that no rain would fall "except by my word" (1 Kings 17:1). When the two men met, there had been no rain for three years. When the king saw the prophet, he yelled, "Is it you, you troubler of Israel?" (1 Kings 18:17).

Elijah hurled back an answer: "I have not troubled Israel; but you have, and your father's house, because you have forsaken the commandments of the LORD . . ." (v. 18).

To speak so forcefully to the king was a bold act, but the prophet did it. Not only was Ahab wicked, but he and his wife both died horrible deaths. There's nothing good ever said about either one of them in the Bible.

This proverb then really says what we all know. We get out of life about what we put into it. If we express those small, almost insignificant acts of kindness, we benefit others. That's always rewarding. But the other side is that something—perhaps mystical—happens to us when we do those deeds. We are enriched, blessed, changed. Conversely, those who harden themselves or ignore others are the real losers. Most people wouldn't think of it as cruelty not to help a neighbor with a flat tire. Perhaps cruelty is too strong. Maybe it's indifference.

When we become indifferent to those needs around us—and I don't even extend this to the distant lands or the overwhelming needs in war-ravaged nations—others being indifferent to us are really paying that indifference back.

It takes little effort to be kind. Such a simple idea, isn't it?

Modern Proverb: *It takes little effort to be kind, and we benefit from being kind to others.*

Watch It!

*When you sit down to eat with a ruler, observe carefully
what is before you, and put a knife to your throat if you
have a big appetite. Do not desire the ruler's delicacies,
for they are deceptive food.*

Proverbs 23:1–3

"I watch the way the person eats. That tells me a great deal about
him or her," said the CEO of a large corporation. As part of a
book I was writing about him, I asked how he promoted people
to the executive level, especially with his rapidly expanding
company.

When the company opened new branches, the CEO asked
the personnel department to narrow the decision down to three
people. "Then I arrange lunch on three successive days," he
said. "Applicants don't realize it, but the way they eat deter-
mines their future."

"Such as?" I said as I sat across from him at lunch.

"You didn't add any salt to your food before you tasted it,
did you?"

I shook my head. "How would I know if it needed it until I
took a bite?"

"Exactly." He smiled and sipped his Perrier. "Those who
salt before tasting tend to be incautious people. They make
rash decisions before they have the necessary information."

He gave me other things he observed about applicants that
included the amount of food they ate, the speed at which they
ate, how much they left on their plates, as well as their food
choices, especially when it came to dessert. "Always listen to
what they say before they choose," he said. "It speaks a great
deal about them."

That was one of the most fascinating interviews I've ever
conducted. It worked with his corporation because he was an

intuitive person. He understood what he called "behavior signals."

The advice from these three verses may have come from the same kind of shrewd observer. As many scholars assume, these were words of advice to young men who were going to serve as courtiers or attendants for a king. They needed to heed them as warnings about the occupational hazards—because service for royalty was both rewarding and dangerous. Such attendants could rise to high office, but plummet to the ground just as easily—everything depended on the king's attitude toward them.

Table manners, the sages say, can bring an attendant to grief. Faced with a sumptuous spread, the temptation for some is to grab for all the good things. It's a lure to express unconscious greed—when all the food is set before them—especially when their eyes stare at a greater variety than they've seen before. They could easily cast aside all restraint and heap their plates high with more food than they would ever eat in a single meal. The elegant surroundings and being in the presence of the powerful could cause them to be awed. Some would lose their appetite, but others—and these are the ones who get warned in these verses—would overeat.

Ingesting huge amounts speaks of their overindulgence. The sages say, "If you're tempted to do that, put a knife to your throat." They probably meant that any display of gluttony is suicidal, and this may be a colorful way of saying "Curb your appetite" or "Show self-restraint." The wise eat with restraint and remain fully aware of the host and the conversation.

This, then, is first of all a series of advice about self-restraint at the table. If we think of it the way the CEO does, it may say much more to us. I'll go a little further and say that everything we do tells something about us—the way we walk, our posture, our choice of clothing colors and styles, even our cars.

This may also speak about maturity. The more mature we are, the more we realize that the things we wanted so badly and couldn't live without aren't very important. Sometimes by holding back and resisting indulging inducements, we may come out ahead.

Temptation—by its nature—is always attractive. I don't know anyone who did something wrong or evil and said, "I knew it was evil." Usually, they'll tell us that the temptation would do something positive for them. Those who murder plan to profit in some way from the deed. It's the same with telling a simple lie.

The more we indulge ourselves, the easier it is to abandon self-restraint.

I see this a lot during the Christmas season. People let go and give in to overeating and ignore all the rules of good nutrition. They do it because they want to feel good, to eat what they consider the forbidden foods, and push away self-restraint. One version says, "Don't go and stuff yourself! That would be the same as cutting your throat. Don't be greedy for all that fancy food!" (CEV).

Temptation constantly surrounds us. We may not be sitting at the table with a king or facing a promotion, but we're also in the presence of God, the One who knows and sees all. Although this proverb has many implications, it certainly urges us to restrain ourselves.

But I wonder if this isn't a subtle way of pushing the readers toward self-examination—a way of saying something like this: "When you're with important people, of course, you'll watch yourself. You won't do anything stupid or misbehave." Just possibly, such words can also cause those same people to look inward and ask, "What makes me greedy? What makes me yearn for the delicacies?"

Such a warning may have brought about better results than if the sages had directly commanded them to exercise self-discipline. That's not surprising, really, when we remember that these writers were the wise people of their day.

Modern Proverb: *Examine yourself. Let the way you act toward people—important and not so important—show who you really are.*

A New Slavery

The rich rule over the poor, and the borrower is the slave of the lender.

Proverbs 22:7

The first time I met Roger, his health had deteriorated, and he worked in a place where everyone smoked—long before companies acknowledged secondhand smoke and office pollution. His company had fine health insurance, but the year I met him, it was his third trip to the hospital for a lung infection and upper respiratory ailments. Roger was fifty-seven years old, and he didn't like his job anyway.

"Why don't you quit?"

"I couldn't get a job that would pay that much," he said. "Besides, I've still got a big mortgage, and I want to get it paid off in the next five years."

That was Roger's choice. Not only was he in debt, but he was enslaved to a job he detested and to a company he didn't like, and his body was paying the price.

I link Roger and people like him to this proverb. The word translated *slave* represents a person under obligation to another, which could also be an employee or the subjects of a king. So the term is appropriate. Although it makes no moral judgments, the verse points out a reality—those who borrow are slaves. That, in itself, should be enough to make us hesitate before asking for a loan. But more than that, we need to ask: What does it really say to us today about the matter of borrowing and lending?

Most of us owe money. It's rare to find people who pay cash for their automobiles; I don't know anyone who plunked down cash for the entire cost of a house. We live in a society that cries out, "Want now, pay later."

Such a proverb reminds me of the early 1990s, when we lived on the east side of Louisville, Kentucky. That particular area had become the affluent neighborhood in which to buy land and build. We lived one block from the invisible line that thrust people into the upper echelon of housing.

I never thought much about the burgeoning community with its immense three-story dwellings. Then one day when I was out running, I noticed one house, about twice the size of our quite-adequate home. People had moved in months earlier, but I still saw no drapes or evidence of any furniture in the front room. I probably wouldn't have thought any more about it except that twice I had seen furniture trucks pulled up in front of the house and furniture being unloaded.

I mentioned the odd appearance of the house to a real estate agent. "Don't you know what's going on?" the agent said.

Obviously, I didn't.

"A lot of us started out married life in tiny houses, with junk furniture and second-rate dishes, and we gradually built up," the agent said. "Not these people—they have to have the top-quality brands and have it now." She explained that the couple both worked full time and were making mortgage payments of $2,000 to $3,000 a month. "They're not high-level professionals, and they're not pulling in a lot of money, so they pay the mortgage and furnish maybe one bedroom. When they want to entertain, they rent the furniture."

I could hardly believe it, but she had already sold houses to three such couples.

"What happens if one of them loses a job?"

"They lose everything," she said. "And it happens."

I saw what could have been that experience enacted the first week we put our house on the market. Ours was a middle-class house that we had fixed up. Although we had added a detached two-car garage and a back deck, our house ranked far below the newer houses in size and amenities. We got an offer the second day, and the couple made a down payment. We began to pack.

Less than two weeks later, the wife lost her job. That's when we learned the precariousness of the situation. The husband

and wife had barely scraped up enough money for a down payment—and that included borrowing from her parents. The wife had no idea when she'd find a new job. On his salary alone, they couldn't handle monthly payments, so they asked us to release them from their contract, which we did.

I've seen this trend in many areas of life. People with this attitude want the best and don't want to wait for it. It's an attitude like that my friend Dixie once talked about: "We want everything instantly. Even the microwave is too slow today."

I've heard a few restraining voices in Christian finance who plead, "Get out of debt now. Don't buy a car on credit. Pay off your house mortgage as quickly as you can." I'm not sure many people listen.

I do know that the people who are heavily indebted are under tremendous amounts of pressure. I also know a lot of people who live from one paycheck to the next. I've learned that they're the people who keep getting inundated with opportunities for increased credit lines.

Last year I learned the name for those of us who pay off our credit card balances each month. We're called deadbeats. It means that Visa or MasterCard won't make a lot of profit off our purchases. Maybe it also means that we've prepared our own emancipation proclamation. We're going to be free to live and to enjoy our lives without being controlled by what we owe.

I don't want to tell anyone what to do, but there is one clear New Testament exhortation that we would do well to pay attention to. In Romans 12 and 13, Paul gives a litany of practical advice that begins with treating our bodies as God's holy temples. As he goes down the list, he writes, "Owe no one anything, except to love one another; for the one who loves another has fulfilled the law" (13:8).

In a subtle way, he speaks against owing people anything of material value. If pushed, he might have said, "You borrow and get into the habit of it, and you become the slave of the lender. Then you can't quit—the lender owns your life."

Too often one debt leads to another to another to another. It's not my intention to tell anyone not to go into debt. What I think we need to consider is where debt leads. It's more than paying money. Debts easily sap our energy, keep us worried and anxious, and may even force us to take on a second job or work extra hours. And maybe we need to ask if having more is worth it.

I have a friend who wanted to make the best living situation for his family, so he worked eighty hours a week for two years. He's divorced now, but his former wife has a great house! His kids are moving into their teen years and they hardly know him. Without realizing it, my friend had become a slave, and it wasn't worth the price he paid.

There's one other thing that strikes me about this proverb—borrowing may be a way for people to shirk responsibility. Going into debt and staying in debt may well indicate a lack of self-discipline and control.

"Credit is the voice of greed," said one of my friends. "Because credit is easy to get, it keeps pushing us to want more and crave for the best when good is adequate."

That makes a lot of sense.

And here's my final thought on the matter of debt. Could it be that those who constantly remain in debt may be seeking satisfaction, inner peace, and meaningful existence in the wrong realms? If they have enough things, doesn't that prove their value to themselves and to others? Is it possible that what they don't find through their commitment to Jesus Christ they must seek elsewhere?

Modern Proverb: *When we go into anyone's debt, that person is in control of our lives.*

All in a Good Name

*A good name is to be chosen rather than great riches,
and favor is better than silver or gold.*

Proverbs 22:1

"You spoiled my name!"

That's the strongest accusation I ever heard during my years of living in Africa. When someone spoke ill of another—and especially when the accused person believed the charge was wrong or unjust—they called it *spoiling* a person's name. The Western world has invaded and changed much of the African culture, but in earlier times, spoiling a person's name was the worst insult someone could hurl at another.

Behind this proverb of choosing a good name lies the ancient Hebrew thought that, more than a label, a name expressed the inner nature and character of the person. To change a name meant a change of the person's character. For example, Jacob, a name that means *deceiver,* had an all-night experience with an angel of Yahweh at the River Jabbok. Before departing, the angel changed his name to Israel. "You shall no longer be called Jacob, but Israel, for you have striven with God and with humans, and have prevailed" (Genesis 32:28). Israel means "one who strives or prevails with God."

In Proverbs, the concept of the good name lies behind words such as *honor* or *favor*—this proverb says that "favor is better than silver or gold." Favor carries the idea of the acceptance and approval of God and of other people. Honor meant respect and esteem and the influence that person exerted within the community. Take the example of Job. Before the calamities struck and overpowered his life, the people held him in high honor, as he points out in Job 29.

179

A good name that surpasses the value of riches isn't in the name alone, because it might be undeserved. The real value of the good name is one that corresponds to the true character and worth of its bearer.

Today people can change their names or move to new locations. Such freedom was rarely available in the closed Old Testament communities, where most people lived all their lives among the same people. They couldn't easily escape their reputations, and their mistakes or bad character followed them and their children and their children's children. That made having a good name even more important in that culture—it was part of the heritage left to their offspring.

It's easy to see that a good name didn't limit itself to reputations and that people spoke well of individuals while they lived—important as having a good name was. The name was understood as an immortal part of individuals—something that survived beyond death. Israelites hoped to be remembered for the good deeds they had done and that their names would endure permanently. They believed in the survival of the name, and the name represented a prolongation of life and was, therefore, quite important. Wealth and possessions don't last, but the memory of a person does.

As I've thought about the significance of having a "good name," I wonder if it's something we're aware of. Is it possible that having a good name may be something of which we're not really conscious? My concern is that those who focus on having a spotless reputation can easily get caught up in trying to say the right things to the right people at the right time and not really be themselves.

Because they focus on the impact they make, they do the one thing that will destroy a good name. Instead of living the kind of life that wins favor and provides them with true honor, they put making their reputation first. In fact, I suspect those who are the most honored may be the ones least aware of the impact they make on others. They may not have that elusive thing called fame or win polls for popularity. But perhaps, in their own ways of living as they do, they may be having a more significant impact.

As I wrote that, I remembered a survey done at our church among our high school youth. They were asked, "Without listing the pastor, who in this church is the Christian you'd most like to be?"

They overwhelmingly named Anne Dunivin, a woman then in her mid-sixties. I smiled when I heard the response, because I knew Anne well. She speaks her mind—sometimes a bit strongly—and she's just as quick to say, "Oh, I'm so sorry, I was wrong." One thing I know about Anne (and others who fit her profile) is that she wasn't trying to make her name important. She was too busy doing her best to please God now.

And when we stop to think about it, isn't that how we build a good name? Just by being true to ourselves? People recognize reality—at least most of the time. Some individuals can fake it and may even deceive, but there's something about "real" people that sets them apart.

Here's an example of what I mean, and I'm not at liberty to use the man's name. The teacher of an adult Sunday school class, he asked the members to pay the school fees for one lower-caste child for one year in India. They not only paid for one child, but they also collected enough money for seven children. A year later, the class decided that instead of giving the teacher an annual Christmas present, they would send money to India for more children. For several weeks, they passed an envelope around and collected almost a thousand dollars.

When they presented the check to the teacher, tears filled his eyes. After pulling himself together, he thanked them for their warmth and love.

At the end of the class, one of the members came to him and said, "I heard what you said about being warm and loving. You don't get it, though, do you?"

"What do you mean?"

"They're only reflecting you."

Isn't that the nicest compliment teachers or individuals could have to show their influence and impact?

Modern Proverb: *If our lifestyle honors our name, we please God. Pleasing God is better than any material possession.*

Loving Friends

A friend loves at all times, and a brother is born for adversity.

Proverbs 17:17, NIV

Some friends play at friendship but a true friend sticks closer than one's nearest kin.

Proverbs 18:24

"You just can't depend on your friends," Terry said with a sharpness in his voice. "When the going gets tough, the friends run away." He went on to complain about how betrayed and let down he felt because he couldn't depend on anyone. We ate lunch and, between mouthfuls of food, he recounted the perfidious attitude and action of those he had counted on and who failed him.

I didn't say much during the hour we spent together. Mostly I listened as he told me story after story, and I knew most of the people he talked about.

"So what do you think?" he asked. "Do you think I ought to give up on friendship?"

His question caught me off guard and I blurted out, "Maybe you need to be a friend if you want a friend."

If I had punched him in the stomach, Terry couldn't have looked more surprised. "But—but I have been, I mean I am—" he sputtered. Obviously, my words weren't what he wanted to hear, and he left angry at me.

As I watched his car drive away, I thought, *I'm sure he'll find people to listen as he tells them how much he had depended on Cec, who not only let him down, but turned against him.*

Terry is one of those sad people—and I think of them as sad—who've never experienced true friendship. He doesn't know the peace, joy, and encouragement that come from a healthy relationship with others. The best he can grasp about friendship is that if he needs someone, he expects their affirmation and encouragement. I don't know anyone to whom Terry has given that kind of support.

On an earlier occasion we talked about friendship and he said, "Yeah, we probably need friends, but I find I can generally do without them." I understood that now.

For me, friendships mean a lot. And when I speak of friends, I refer to the individuals I truly care about and know they care about me.

Through the years, I've collected aphorisms that express the way friendships function—at least the kind of friendships I want. Here's a sampling:

- A loyal friend laughs at your jokes when they're not so good, and sympathizes with your problems when they're not so bad. —Arnold H. Glasow
- A friend is a person with whom I may be sincere. Before him I may think aloud. —Ralph Waldo Emerson
- Friends are angels who lift us to our feet when our wings have trouble remembering how to fly. —Anonymous
- A friend hears the song in my heart and sings it to me when my memory fails. —Anonymous

God never intended for one person to stand alone or be alone. By our innate nature we need people, even if some need them less than others. The point of Proverbs 17:17 is that when trouble hits us, we reach out. Our friends are there—we assume—and sometimes those friends are more loving and accepting than our nearest relative.

All through Proverbs, the sages use the common word for friend (Hebrew *rea*), which also means *neighbor* or *comrade*, depending on the context. Although the sages didn't say it, I'm sure they'd agree that it's better to have a few close friends than a lot of acquaintances.

Doesn't Jesus set the example? Crowds constantly followed him, but he related to twelve. The most private and troublesome times he spent with only three—Peter, James, and John.

When Proverbs speaks of friends, loyalty or constancy seems to be the strongest feature emphasized. Not only is it implicit that we have friends who are closer than a relative or who love us all the time, but it's also a way of exhorting us to be that kind of friend to others.

It is interesting that the strongest word in the Old Testament for a friend (*allup,* literally, a *bosom companion*) usually occurs in situations of betrayal (see Proverbs 2:17) or estrangement (as in 16:28 and chap. 17). It's as if the sage reminds us that we need to nurture and guard the closest friendship.

Above, I listed a few aphorisms, but here is my own definition of a friend: A true friend knows all your faults, still loves you, and has no plan for your self-improvement. The last phrase in particular explains genuine friendship.

A true friend accepts me as I am. Perhaps that sounds so simple and obvious, but too many relationships are built around what I call Repair Connections. They're committed to fixing up one another—that is, making them whole as they perceive the other's inadequacies. They're the kind who tell us things "for your own good."

By contrast, and as I've mentioned elsewhere, David Morgan has been my friend for more than twenty years, and perhaps a dozen years ago he moved into the sacred spot of being my best friend. I put him there because I'm convinced he cares about me, no matter whether I improve, grow, or regress in my life. He's there for me and genuinely loves me. Obviously, I feel the same about David.

Here's the one thing my friendship with David has taught me. In not trying to repair me or to make me better, he accepted me with all my obvious shortcomings. By loving the unlovable parts of me, he did something that other relationships haven't done—he made me want to grow and to get rid of at least some of those blemishes in my life.

In fact, when I think about David, in some ways he models the friendship I have with Jesus Christ. I know Jesus wants me to be perfect and pure, but I don't get spiritual e-mail messages to tell me how badly I've failed. What I do see is the one who says, "My burden is light. Let me help carry yours too." He loves me and accepts me, and that acceptance becomes exactly what I need to become a person who pleases God in every way.

Isn't it marvelous how true friendship works?

Modern Proverb: *Be a friend if you want a friend. True friends are there for us in our times of joy and in sorrow.*

Getting Revenge

Do not rejoice when your enemies fall, and do not let your heart be glad when they stumble, or else the LORD will see it and be displeased, and turn away his anger from them.

Proverbs 24:17–18

It was one of those true stories that I wish I had documented and kept in my files so that I'd retain the names and dates. I saw it on one of the nightly national news segments on TV. In a bungled robbery, a young man murdered another man of about the same age. The police caught the killer and he confessed. Somehow the mother of the slain son got permission to visit the murderer in prison.

"You took the life of my son and I have no other," she said, "so now you must be my son. My heart is sad, but I forgive you and will treat you as I would have treated him."

What a powerful story of love! What grace—far beyond any I've ever seen. I knew one murderer—a woman who was convicted and executed—and before she died she tried to receive forgiveness from the families of her victims. They spoke out about her horrific crime and said she was only trying to get her sentence commuted.

I knew the woman well because a publisher had authorized me to write her story. She was ready to die, and I believe her desire for forgiveness was genuine. What an opportunity, I thought, for those three families of the murdered victims to express grace and forgiveness, but so far as I know, none of them did. Part of the sadness of it all was that the families appeared at the trial every day—along with their pastors. One church group even demonstrated outside the courtroom, demanding the death penalty.

That's probably about the worst, most unforgiving attitude

I've ever seen toward enemies. I don't understand that kind of hardness. True, I've not had any family member murdered. If I had, I'd like to believe that, with God's help, I could move beyond my deep pain and forgive.

Doesn't being a disciple of Jesus Christ mean we emulate his behavior and cry out, "Father, forgive them; for they do not know what they are doing" (Luke 23:34)?

I know of one woman who expressed that kind of forgiveness. I was teaching in India in January 1999 when I read the report of the death of an Australian missionary and his two young sons. Apparently, while they were sleeping in a vehicle, religious extremists burned them alive.

In February 2000, I had returned to India and learned they had captured the murderer. The next day, the missionary's widow was interviewed on TV. She made it clear that she was glad they had captured the man so that he would not kill again. With her arms around her daughter and only surviving child, she looked into the camera and said, "I forgive him for what he's done."

I've given the most extreme cases, of course, and something most of us won't have to face. Maybe we need to think about more minor matters. What about the little incidents where people offend us? Speak against us? Cheat us? Lie about us?

Revenge isn't the answer. In fact, we're told not to attempt revenge: "Beloved, never avenge yourselves, but leave room for the wrath of God; for it is written, 'Vengeance is mine, I will repay, says the Lord'" (Romans 12:19). In other words, that's God's special department. Too often we gloat when people we don't like have bad times, get fired, or go through a divorce. "Serves them right," we say.

Even though we're told not to gloat over the misfortunes of others, I don't see that as the same as shouting victory as the Israelites did in what is called the Song of Moses (Exodus 15) after the destruction of the pursuing Egyptian army. This is really a matter of attitude. We praise God for victories—and that often entails another's loss or defeat. The proverb's exhortation has more to do with the enemies we live around and work among—the people we dislike or who irritate us—than it does with our triumphs.

The New Testament takes this a step further: ". . . Love your enemies and pray for those who persecute you," said Jesus (Matthew 5:44). But even there, the emphasis is on that all-out kind of persecution or attempt to destroy us. That's not what most of us live with.

I think of David, who spent years running away from Saul. If the king had captured him, that would have been the end of David's life. When Saul died in the final battle, David wept for his enemy. He wept when his rebellious son Absalom died—the one who had usurped the throne and wanted his father dead. For me, David's ability to weep for his enemies shows me why God regarded him so highly despite his human failings.

Ours is a much pettier world, where we rarely have life-and-death situations. Ours are struggles with jealousy, greed, irritation, and competition. The real test comes when we apply the words of Romans 12:15: "Rejoice with those who rejoice, weep with those who weep."

Whenever others—even the people we don't like very much—have serious illness or great tragedy, most of us are sensitive enough to feel sympathy for them. But what about when they succeed? Can we rejoice over their success?

I think that's the test for us. If we can genuinely and honestly say "Congratulations" over someone else's success, then we're close to a modern application of the ancient proverb.

Modern Proverb: *Rejoice with others who succeed. When you do, you please God.*

Strife Makers

*Like the glaze covering an earthen vessel are smooth lips
with an evil heart. An enemy dissembles in speaking while
harboring deceit within; when an enemy speaks graciously, do not believe it, for there are seven abominations
concealed within; though hatred is covered with guile, the
enemy's wickedness will be exposed in the assembly.*

Proverbs 26:23–26

Although it's been six years since the incident, I still vividly
remember the strife maker. His name is Bob, and we were part
of a group of Christians who went to Nicaragua to help build a
house for a national pastor. Because we were there without our
mates, they housed us together.

During the day, Bob was genial and hardworking, but when
we relaxed at night I saw another side of him. Long after dark
on the third workday, we were lying on our narrow beds when
he began to complain about something that had happened—an
incident that hadn't bothered me. He kept explaining (and complaining) and before long I agreed with him. He brought up two
more things that "just weren't right," and by the time we went
to sleep, I was upset and slept badly. Bob slept fine—or at least
his snoring indicated that he had.

The next day at our staff meeting, I brought up the very
things that Bob had complained about so vigorously. No one
else seemed disturbed. "What about you, Bob?" I asked. "You
brought it up last night and—"

"Me?" he shrugged. "I'm all right."

His show of indifference shocked me so badly, I didn't say
anything. I told the group to forget it. That very night, Bob
started to complain, so I said, "If this disturbs you, why don't
you tell the whole staff? I don't want to hear it."

Bob never complained to me again; he never talked to the
staff either. However, he did begin to talk with one of the
single women. She was a little smarter than I was. In a staff

meeting, she said, "Bob has been quite unhappy, and I think he needs to speak up."

An embarrassed Bob denied he was upset or that he had complained.

Obviously, I don't know Bob's heart, but he's what I call a strife maker. I don't think he does it intentionally, but it's like a gift. Quite unconsciously, he has a way of stirring people up, upsetting them, or making them angry over things that wouldn't ordinarily give them concern. Yet when confronted, he denies any negative feelings.

Most of the time, strife makers disguise themselves with their words, but their hearts harbor deceit. Like Bob, they can be charming individuals.

Let's look more closely at strife makers. Verse 23 says, "Like the glaze covering an earthen vessel are smooth lips with an evil heart." The writers refer to a common practice of that day. People dipped their pottery into glaze to make the objects smooth, shiny, and more attractive. The pots themselves weren't particularly attractive, so they put on the outer glaze—the veneer—to make them more appealing. The sages then compare shiny pots with the lips of the evil-hearted. Their point? Hypocrisy of the lips is like a veneer laid over an evil heart.

One of the problems in dealing with such people is that they often present a warm or cheery appearance—at first—and hide their true nature. The description of them reminds me of Jesus' rebuke of the Pharisees. They were supposedly the pious and the holy who meticulously observed the literal law whenever possible. Jesus called them "whitewashed tombs" (Matthew 23:27). While they may have been white on the outside, they were still the place of death. Despite the Pharisees' seemingly pious attitudes, their piety was only a veneer.

These verses in Proverbs also speak about the malicious who hide behind charming speech or clever words. They show one thing on the outside while being something else inside. By conveying a false impression, they hope to achieve their sinister or selfish objectives.

There's another kind of strife maker that we need to look at.

They're the people who always have turmoil and strife around them. They go from one major crisis to another. The first time I became aware of this, my friend Chuck was talking about his mother: "When there weren't any problems, she found a way to stir things up." Chuck came from a family of seven, and his mother would go to one sibling and say, "Did you know what your brother said?" And of course, the saying would always be negative and cause problems.

One thing Chuck finally figured out about his mother was that she wasn't happy. "How can she ever be at peace when things are in turmoil around her all the time?" he said.

What I observed about her was that when chaos and strife raged, she felt "normal." To stay feeling normal in quiet times, on quite an unconscious level, she stirred things up.

The sages write: ". . . when an enemy speaks graciously, do not believe it, for there are seven abominations concealed within . . ." (v. 25). *Seven abominations* probably means that the hatred or strife is the spawning ground for any number of wicked thoughts and actions. Verse 26 adds that sooner or later the duplicity and treachery will be exposed. Unfortunately, they usually have done the damage—which is how they're finally exposed.

Before I finished this chapter, I wondered a little more about strife makers. That is, I wondered how they feel about themselves. The Pharisees, for example, surely didn't see themselves as evil or they surely would have changed.

Is it possible to be so blinded by our prejudices and our understanding of life that we're quite intolerant of other viewpoints? For example, I have an acquaintance who calls himself a liberal and espouses what others would call the far-left positions. Despite all that man's statements about being liberal and open, he's as narrow in his position as those he speaks against. He's just intolerant in a different way. And he's a strife maker because he constantly asserts that his viewpoint is the same as God's.

Maybe being a strife maker has to do with recognizing only what we choose to see—our own viewpoint—and refusing to acknowledge others' perceptions.

Maybe it means we all need to do a lot of serious self-examining to make certain *we* are not strife makers!

Modern Proverb: *Those who stir up others—no matter how cleverly they do so—eventually get found out and people learn the truth.*

PART FOUR

Living with Business and Law

Lies and Laws

Whoever speaks the truth gives honest evidence, but a false witness speaks deceitfully.

Proverbs 12:17

A faithful witness does not lie, but a false witness breathes out lies.

Proverbs 14:5

The first part of the story is really laughable, and then it turns tragic. King Ahab wanted to enlarge his holdings, so he offered to buy a plot of ground from a man named Naboth. The owner, whose land was near the king's palace, refused to sell. After all, the land had been in his family countless generations.

The disappointed king went home and sulked. "He lay down on his bed, turned away his face, and would not eat" (1 Kings 21:4).

The first time I read those words, I laughed out loud. The king acted like a spoiled child because he couldn't have what he wanted. So he pouted and then, worse, he went into depression. That's where the story turns tragic.

Queen Jezebel hired two scoundrels to accuse Naboth of blasphemy, and the penalty was death. For the death penalty to be enacted, the Law of Moses required "two or three witnesses." Jezebel had the right number, and they swore, "Naboth cursed God and the king" (1 Kings 21:13). The people stoned Naboth, and immediately afterward King Ahab grabbed possession of the land.

The death of Naboth didn't happen merely on the word of two men, but they went through the legal proceedings. In the cities and towns of Israel, the courts met at the gates of the city, which in this case was Samaria. Elders—that is, a number of the leading citizens—took on the role of judges. Supposedly, they listened impartially when accusations came against individuals in criminal and civil cases.

195

Then, every bit as much as today, the verdict often depended on the truthfulness of the witnesses. Most of the time when the Old Testament refers to lies, telling the truth, or bearing witness, the writers have in mind this picture of the ancient judicial system.

Likewise, in the Ten Commandments, when the Bible says, "You shall not bear false witness against your neighbor" (Exodus 20:16), that's the intent of the command—not to lie under oath. This is the worst form of lying, because it mocks justice and can lead to the wrongful sentencing of an innocent person. The Ninth Commandment refers to deliberately lying against an innocent person. Although bad enough, it wasn't aimed against lying to help cover the crime of the guilty. Until such a commandment, anyone could charge someone with a crime and whoever had the most influence won.

Proverbs 14:25 says it well: "A truthful witness saves lives, but one who utters lies is a betrayer."

We get a sense of the seriousness of this when we think of the towns and cities where such justice took place. These were small communities, where everyone probably knew everyone else and they had lived there for generations.

The worst thing about bearing false witness—in the sense of speaking a lie or making charges against an innocent person—is that it ruins the reputation of those who don't deserve it.

Although these are legal issues of truth telling and bring to mind a courtroom setting, the principle carries far beyond the law. In one sense, every minute of the day, we're living witnesses of the grace of God. When we speak truthfully, we're faithful witnesses. When we lie or deceive or misrepresent facts, it could be said of us ". . . a false witness breathes out lies."

To carry this a little further, sometimes our lies are only exaggerations or embellishments. I recall once being at a party where two people had a difference of opinion. Neither was willing to back down, and the verbal assaults became stronger for perhaps a minute, certainly no longer.

A few days later, one of them recounted the incident to a small group of us at lunch. As he recited the part about "I said . . ." and "then he said . . ." I began to wonder if it was the same disagreement I had overheard. The storyteller's recital made his own words sound much softer than I had remembered them—and his opponent's much sharper than what I had heard.

Was he lying? Yes, I think so. Did he know he was lying? Ah, there I honestly don't know. Perhaps he was so intent to prove something that he didn't mind stretching the truth (or exaggerating) about what actually happened.

Writing about being a witness in a court of law isn't that different, is it? When people lie under oath, isn't it out of selfishness—a desire to protect themselves, to get even, or to punish? I wonder if telling lies that belittle or accuse others isn't as serious as being a dishonest witness in a court of law.

Or at least, I wonder if God considers it that way. As I wonder, it also makes me pause and look at my own words about others. How many times have I misrepresented another person? I'd love to say, "Never."

But I wonder if that too would be a lie.

Modern Proverb: *Lies hurt other people. In the long run, they also hurt the liars themselves. If we always tell the truth, everyone wins.*

Rashly Responding

*Do you see someone who is hasty in speech? There is
more hope for a fool than for anyone like that.*

Proverbs 29:20

Henry Nyakwana offered me friendship and guidance the first
day we met in Kenya, East Africa. Among other things, he
pushed me in learning the language by refusing to speak to me
in English. Carefully, he explained tribal customs, taught me to
bargain in the open-air markets, and treated me the way he
would have treated any African.

Only once did a problem arise between us. A preacher
named Nashon visited me and we chatted a few minutes. "I
suppose you have not heard what Henry is saying about you?"
he asked.

"What do you mean?"

"He's plotting to get rid of you."

"I don't believe that!"

"See. Doesn't that show how cleverly he has deceived you?"

I pushed Nashon to give me details, which he did. As I listened, a storm raged within me. My dearest African friend had
betrayed me—or the person I had thought was a friend. He had
deceived me. What a fool I had been.

Enraged over the betrayal, I lashed out and said, "I'm going
to face him right now."

"Oh, do not say anything of this," Nashon said. "I have told
you because I am your friend, and you need to know."

I couldn't promise my silence, even though he begged.
"Right now I'm too upset to talk any longer." I left Nashon and
went for a long walk on the nearby mountain trail.

An hour later I returned, still angry. To calm myself, I wrote

198

a letter and asked someone to deliver it to Henry in person—I was too hurt to look into his eyes and accuse him. In essence, I said, "If you don't want me here, just say so and I'll leave. It hurts me deeply that you would act that way behind my back. I believed you were my friend."

Minutes later, Henry was at my door. "Who has told you such lies? Do you not know me better than that? Do you not know that I love you and would never speak against you? Are you not my special friend?"

Pain blazed in his eyes, and I raced across the room and hugged him. I apologized and he forgave me.

During those moments, I realized three painful facts. First, Nashon had lied to me. Second, Henry had never done anything hurtful to me in the three years we had worked together. The pain on his face erased any doubt that might have existed. Third, and the most powerful lesson, I had acted stupidly—I had believed a lie.

The next day, both of us confronted Nashon, who tried to squirm out of his words by saying that he had "heard it spoken by others," but he wouldn't give us a single name.

"Why would you believe Nashon?" Henry asked when we were alone. "Do you not know that he wishes to take my place? He has spread *fatina* (gossip) about me for a long time and at every opportunity."

Then I thought about it. Yes, on two previous occasions he had belittled Henry. I hadn't paid much attention. Now I wish I had defended Henry.

"I want to make you a promise," I said. "If I ever hear anyone speak one word against you again—the slightest accusation—I will come directly to you and ask you." Until his death twenty years later, Henry remained one of my special friends.

Although that experience took place many years ago, I remember it vividly—not just for the lessons I learned, but because I had deeply wounded someone who deserved only my love and appreciation. I acted like a fool because I had listened to a lie and accepted the words. As painful as that experience was to me, I learned a great deal.

It also reminded me what the Old Testament says about accusations: "A single witness shall not suffice to convict a person of any crime or wrongdoing in connection with any offense that may be committed. Only on the evidence of two or three witnesses shall a charge be sustained" (Deuteronomy 19:15).

Years later when I was a pastor, one prominent couple in the church started passing on rumors or making accusations against other members. They never made them directly, but they prefaced their sneak attacks with "People are saying . . ." or "There are some members who say . . ."

At first I listened to them and probably believed some of their words. But over a period of months, I began to wonder how accurate the charges were and why they felt they had to tell me.

One day, I read Deuteronomy 19:15 aloud and said, "From now on, don't tell me what 'they' are saying. If you're going to pass on any complaint against anyone, I want to know the name of the person who told you. Otherwise, don't tell me."

They never made another accusation.

Words have tremendous power for good or ill, so it's easy to understand why the sages wrote many statements about the power of speech, especially when it came to accusing others. Almost every chapter in this book has something to say about the kind of speech that gets people into trouble and the kind that is helpful.

Proverbs makes many suggestions about the use of the tongue. Restraint in speech is one of the most common. Those who speak rashly, who pour forth words before they have given themselves a chance to think, will get into trouble. Words, once spoken, can't be recalled any more than bullets can be returned to a gun once fired. Abraham Lincoln is usually credited with saying, "Better to remain silent and be thought a fool than to speak out and remove all doubt."

Another useful piece of advice I heard in childhood was, "Give everyone your ear, but your voice to few."

In Proverbs, only two kinds of people rank lower than the fool—those who consider themselves wise (26:12) and those who speak rashly, as mentioned here. Talk is cheap, and it can also be insensitive, malicious, foolish, destructive, wasteful, and indiscreet. Those who blurt out anything often cause great harm to others as well as to themselves.

For example, an incident happened as the Jews were in the wilderness wanderings. A man with an Israelite mother and an Egyptian father was accused of blasphemy, for which the penalty was death. So they brought him to Moses to settle the case. Seeing the man and hearing the charge might easily have caused Moses to blow up and say, "Death." He didn't. He had them hold the man in custody until he could hear a decision from God (Leviticus 24:12). After praying, he sentenced the man to die, but it wasn't a rash decision.

As I thought of that story, it reminded me that Moses had once been a hasty man. He angrily killed an Egyptian who had treated a Hebrew badly (Exodus 2:11ff.). The next day when he tried to stop two Hebrews from fighting, one of them asked, "Do you mean to kill me as you killed the Egyptian?" (v. 14).

Fear gripped Moses, and he fled from the land and stayed away forty years until God brought him back. In those years of wandering as a shepherd, apparently the man learned his lesson.

Maybe one of the lessons we need to learn is to apply the Old Testament legal rule to our dealings with others. How much pain could we avoid if we said, "Your word against her isn't enough. Who else says this?"

Modern Proverb: *Don't believe every accusation. Think first. Speak second.*

Making Vows

It is a snare for one to say rashly, "It is holy," and begin to reflect only after making a vow.

Proverbs 20:25

I've made only a handful of vows in my entire life. I've promised, implied, agreed, but for me making a vow has always been the ultimate commitment. I may be making more of the concept of *vow* than most people would. From my perspective, however, whenever I make a vow it is nonretractable and final. I will keep it or die in the process.

Here are three vows I've made in my entire life—and the only three I've made.

The most important was that once-for-all commitment to Jesus Christ; I purposely chose the word *vow*. For at least a year I had seriously considered everything I could find out about God; daily I read the Bible, and finally I knew I believed. I gave my sacred oath that I would follow God the rest of my life.

The reason I took the word *vow* so seriously came about the first time I read Ecclesiastes 5:4–6: "When you make a vow to God, do not delay fulfilling it . . . Fulfill what you vow. It is better that you should not vow than that you should vow and not fulfill it. Do not let your mouth lead you into sin, and do not say before the messenger that it was a mistake; why should God be angry at your words, and destroy the work of your hands?"

My second sacred oath was my marriage vow to Shirley, which meant for me "until death do us part." That's not meant as any kind of indictment of people who go through a divorce. My concept is that for those who take marriage as a sacred vow, breaking it is a last resort and not an easy way out of a relationship.

Third, as I tell elsewhere in this book, I made a vow to God that I would never give less than 15 percent of my income to God. I didn't know much about vows then, although I consciously made a sacred promise to God. Really, it was more of a sacred bargain. If God would provide for my needs, I vowed I would never give less than 15 percent. God hasn't failed me, either.

In the early days after that third vow, I sometimes had trouble paying, especially during those years after our children were born and I was in graduate school. But with God's help I kept that vow.

Promises, on the other hand, mean I've given my word and I'll do my best to fulfill it. My thinking is that I can rescind a promise—by explaining to those I've promised and asking them to release me. Maybe I could do that with a vow, but I like to think of vows as having no escape clauses.

For example, when I promise to visit someone, I have every intention of doing so, but I might also have to call and say, "I'm sorry, I can't come over." When I make a vow, I don't give myself that option.

Despite what I've said, this proverb is more about rash speaking than it is about vows, although certainly both ideas are here. The context shows that it refers to worship and stresses that it binds those who make vows.

In ancient Jewish worship, when people declared, "It is holy," they turned over to Yahweh whatever they had pledged to give. That is, the vowed object became the property of God. So to vow and not to follow through on that sacred commitment was a serious matter.

The Law of Moses put it this way: "When a man makes a vow to the LORD, or swears an oath to bind himself by a pledge, he shall not break his word; he shall do according to all that proceeds out of his mouth" (Numbers 30:2).

Another place says it even stronger: "If you make a vow to the LORD your God, do not postpone fulfilling it; for the LORD your God will surely require it of you, and you would incur guilt. But if you refrain from vowing, you will not incur guilt. Whatever your lips utter you must diligently perform, just as you have freely vowed to the Lord your God with your own mouth" (Deuteronomy 23:21–24).

The sensible advice to anyone is obvious: It's better not to make a sacred promise than to do so and not fulfill that commitment. I've realized that at times people get caught up in the excitement of the moment, and they make the kind of sacred commitments they wouldn't promise under ordinary circumstances. The enthusiasm of the moment doesn't reflect realistic assessment of the ability to carry it out.

For instance, during my first year of college, a fellow student said that he had not earned good grades in high school and didn't think any college would let him in. "I made a vow to God," he said. "Apple pie is my favorite dessert, and I promised God I would never eat apple pie again if a college would accept me."

Frankly, the vow seemed as foolish to me then as it does today, although so far as I know he never touched apple pie. At least, his was a harmless vow.

The one story in the Bible that I consider the most horrific is Jephthah's vow. Although made foolishly, it was a solemn commitment to God and, apparently, he followed through.

The story of his vow appears in Judges 11:29–40. "Then the Spirit of the Lord came upon Jephthah" and he won battles against the Ammonites, but he hadn't fully defeated them. In the excitement of the moment, he made a vow: "If you will give the Ammonites into my hand, then whoever comes out of the doors of my house to meet me when I return victorious from the Ammonites, shall be the Lord's to be offered up by me as a burnt offering" (vv. 30–31).

It was a stupid, horrible thing to say—to vow to burn a human being—but such sacrifices were commonly offered among the pagans around them, so it may not have been so terrible for that culture and time as it sounds today.

When the soldier returned home—in total victory—the first person he saw was his daughter: "She was his only child, he had no son or daughter except her" (v. 34). When he saw her, and although it saddened him, he still felt he had to fulfill the vow he had made.

Surely God would have released Jephthah from his vow, but the man took his promise as sacred. For that consistency, I admire him, although I don't fully understand the culture of that day. I live at least three thousand years later, where I couldn't conceive of anyone sacrificing a child or any other living being.

By contrast, Shirley's parents dedicated her to God—and, for them, that constituted a vow. Thirty years later, when we prepared to leave for Africa, I realized how seriously her mother had taken that commitment: "When Shirley was born," she said, "we surrendered her to God. 'She is yours to do with as you choose,' we said."

When the time came for Shirley and me to leave, she confessed, "I struggled most of the night in prayer over this. Shirley belongs to God, but it took me hours to release her."

As she spoke of the deep struggle, she didn't speak of trying to dissuade God. She had given her daughter to God, and now she had to surrender any hold she had.

Most of us won't make such violent or drastic vows, but each of these stories illustrates that when we promise God, our words become sacred.

Sacred words.

That's what the proverb says. When we vow to God—when we give our solemn oath—let's do it slowly and seriously, and allow ourselves no escape clause.

Modern Proverb: *Don't make a solemn commitment to God until you've thought it through carefully. Once you've made a vow, consider it binding forever.*

Playing Favorites

. . . Partiality in judging is not good.

Proverbs 24:23

To show partiality is not good—yet for a piece of bread a person may do wrong.

Proverbs 28:21

I wonder what Peter thought before he went to the house of the Roman military leader named Cornelius. The wealthy man, part of the detested nation that ruled Israel, had called for the apostle. God tried to prepare Peter by giving him a dream about eating unclean animals and insects and saying to him, "What God has made clean, you must not call profane" (Acts 10:15).

Peter went to the rich man's house and found it filled with Cornelius's friends and relatives. Peter must have finally understood the meaning of the dream because he said, "I truly understand that God shows no partiality . . ." (v. 34).

That must have been an amazing bridge for Peter to cross over. Jews had looked down upon Gentiles and referred to them as dogs. They especially despised Romans because they had conquered the land. But now, face to face with a righteous Roman, all the prejudice fell aside. Peter's words as much as said, "Anyone who turns to God is acceptable."

Despite Peter's understanding of God's grace at work, all believers didn't immediately accept that position. The issue of Gentiles being equal and acceptable in the church raged through most of the first century. The Jews had long seen themselves as the chosen people, and for many that implied that God loved them most. The only way non-Jews could enter into the special relationship with God was to convert and to become Jews first. That moment of Peter's insight with Cornelius changed theology forever.

I've thought about what a shakeup that experience must have brought about in Peter's life. It makes me aware that, even today, being impartial seems to be a problem. Despite the civil rights movement and hundreds of laws, injustice and favoritism still flourish. Laws can only regulate behavior and punish those charged with violating them. No statutes can regulate hearts or attitudes.

Yet we need to seek impartiality if justice is to prevail. One of the major points of the book of Proverbs is that the people who follow God seek justice. Many proverbs praise the just or righteous and give many examples of unjust actions. Justice is given a high place as an example of wise living. I like to define justice as the desire to give what is right or appropriate to others.

Isn't it amazing that most of us cry out when we feel mistreated or discriminated against? Yet we don't seem quite so tenderhearted when we're in the upper position. Too often justice favors the rule of the strong or the wealthy. Justice means that all people in the same situation ought to be treated the same way.

I love the idea of the American symbol of justice—the blindfolded woman holding the scales. If she's going to give what's due and right to everyone, she can't see the person whose case she weighs, and she'll be able to be impartial in her decisions.

Impartiality also means recognizing that each of us is as valuable to God as anyone else. Does that sound too obvious? I wonder.

A few years ago I saw a film in which a harassed and demanding father tried to pressure the family's adult babysitter to cancel her plans and come to work because his wife was out of town and he needed to go away on business. He seemed oblivious to the guests in her home.

After he made several demands, she finally asked, "Is your life more important than mine?"

The man said no, but the audience knew he meant yes. (She didn't leave her guests.)

What a great question: "Is your life more important than mine?" I think that gets to the heart of justice better than anything contemporary that I know.

Here are two examples. I used to ghostwrite the autobi-ographies of famous people. One Christian celebrity headed up several humanitarian programs to help tragedy-stricken people around the world with food, clothing, and especially medical assistance. While working with him on his autobiography, I saw some of those efforts and applauded his work.

I also saw him at his home base. He'd call employees into the office in the middle of the night to do something that prob-ably could have waited until the next day. He'd sometimes be on the phone early in the morning, demanding that they get there immediately because he needed them. No one stood up to him or challenged his demands, except for one secretary. After a month she quit, and the celebrity couldn't understand why. "I paid her well," he said to me, unable to figure it out.

I didn't volunteer the obvious.

Here's another example. One day I was standing in an extremely long line at the post office. A woman rushed up to the front and said, "I'm in a dreadful hurry, please, may I get in front of you?" She was a beautiful young woman, with a soft, sweet voice. The postal worker shrugged and said okay.

However, the person she tried to step in front of said, "Excuse me, but I've waited for this spot. If you want to get to the front of the line, you can do what the rest of us do. You start at the back and work your way forward."

"But I have—"

I couldn't hear her excuse, but she was shocked that he wouldn't let her in. "If I came up to you, would you let me in front of you?" the man said.

"Of course."

"And that means you'd let all these other people in as well." He smiled and said, "So you might as well get to the end of the line like the rest of us."

I think she would have persisted, except several other people then voiced their displeasure.

"I think this is terrible!" she said and stomped out.

Several of us laughed about the incident. One elderly woman said, "She's young and pretty, and I'll bet she gets away with that kind of thing often. What will happen when she reaches fifty?"

"To show partiality is not good—yet for a piece of bread a person may do wrong" needs a brief explanation. It refers to a bribe. Some have said that everyone has a price—if the payoff is big enough, people will steal, lie, or pervert justice. They are those who are so eager to sell themselves that they'll do it for a small amount. In this case, it's a way of saying that some people will sell their integrity and honor for something as insignificant as a crust of bread.

How important are integrity, morality, and honesty? Many obviously think they're worth little. Those who want to live with their integrity, however, won't give in, regardless of the pressure to compromise.

After I had turned eighteen and been one week out of high school, I landed an office job with civil service in the time-keeping division. Everyone had to punch a time card in a machine. One part of the job bothered me. The boss of the whole section was supposed to be there by 8:00, but I never saw him there—ever—before 8:30. I had to be on the job by 7:30, and one of my responsibilities was to punch in his time card.

I wasn't a Christian, but I knew that wasn't right. I complained to Louie, my immediate supervisor. "I've told you your responsibilities. When you punch in your own card, you punch in his."

"It isn't right and I'm not going to do it."

He shrugged. "If you refuse, then don't come back to work tomorrow."

I capitulated and punched the card, although I did wait until right at 8:00 before I punched it, instead of 7:15 when I usually got there. I hated doing it, but I wanted the job. When I finally did leave the job, my final words to Louie were "Just think. I'll never have to cheat for him again."

He shrugged. "Somebody else will."

Looking back, I realize that my bribe wasn't a piece of bread, but it amounted to the same thing.

The saddest thing about the reality of injustice—and it was cheating the government and ultimately all taxpayers that makes it unjust—is that I had done the deed. I suspect that everyone in the building knew what was going on, and we conspired by our silence.

Justice, however, says, "I will speak up, regardless of the consequences." Sometimes the consequences will cost us our jobs and our reputations, but I wonder if maintaining personal integrity isn't more important than holding onto a job. If we give in on one thing, we start the downslide, and when do we yell, "Halt!"?

Isn't integrity the point of this? We want justice for ourselves. We want God to smile on us as much as anyone else. Maybe to get fair treatment, we have to learn to give it first.

Modern Proverb: *No matter what, we need to be true to who we are. That's wisdom. It's also the right thing to do.*

Taking Chances with God

Casting the lot puts an end to disputes and decides between powerful contenders.

Proverbs 18:18

"I didn't know what to do about this decision," Ben said. "It was a once-in-a-lifetime opportunity for me." He had a splendid job-promotion offer that more than doubled his salary, with a number of perks, and it was a position he knew he could handle. However, taking the promotion meant moving more than a thousand miles away. His wife would have to quit her job and relocate.

Ben prayed and so did his wife, Sharon, members of their Sunday school class, and several of their Christian friends. Every day Ben weighed the issue. "Should I say yes or no?" he asked countless times. As the deadline neared for him to give an answer, he felt no more peace about it than he had two weeks earlier when the company made the offer.

Through the ordeal, Ben had tried every method he knew to receive guidance. He had surrendered; he had tried to remove any bias from the situation and pray objectively; he had asked what would be better for him, what would be better for Sharon, what would be better for them as a couple. He wrote a list of positives and negatives, but that didn't seem to help. His friends advised him, but one contradicted the other.

"Sharon didn't want to leave her job," he said, "but if I felt this was right for us, she wouldn't hesitate." He shook his head. "So Sharon couldn't give the answer either."

The day before he had to accept or turn down the position, Ben sat in his office, trying to figure out what to do. "I was getting desperate," he said. "I just didn't know what to do." Then

211

he remembered something from the Old Testament from a Sunday school lesson.

"The Urim and Thummim," he said, when he called me. "How did it work?" (In the Old Testament, beginning with the time of Moses, it became the method for the high priest to determine guidance for the nation.)

"We're not sure, but, most likely, it was a simple thing like having a white stone and a black one inside a bag. At least that seems the most commonly accepted understanding," I said. "After the high priest prayed for God to direct him, as an act of faith, he reached inside the bag and pulled out one of the two stones. He believed God would direct his fingers. If it was white, the answer was yes."

After our conversation, and in acute desperation, Ben decided to try a similar method. Although slightly embarrassed, he handed his secretary two toothpicks. He had broken one of them. He then had her hold out her fist with both ends showing so that he was unable to tell which was longer. He chose one. It was the longer one, which meant yes.

Ben and Sharon moved west. A few months after his relocation, he called me, excited over the way things had worked out. "I honestly believe God guided me through that business with the toothpicks," he said. "I prayed for guidance and my life sure has been better since coming here. Sharon's got the best job she's ever had, and our offices are less than a block apart. We have lunch together two or three times a week—we never had that before."

I'm slightly embarrassed to relate this story because, to those of us in the modern world, the idea sounds strange, even ridiculous. We'd rather refer Ben to his pastor, professional job counselor, or a therapist, or urge him to get on his knees and pray until he knew exactly what the Holy Spirit was saying. Or maybe tell him to read his Bible until a verse spoke to him. All of those methods work at various times.

In ancient times, however, they apparently resorted to the lot to discern God's will.

"Casting of lots? Isn't that something like gambling?" someone asked me in a Bible study group.

"That depends," I said.

I tried to set up scenarios to show the difference. In an ancient court of law, how did they decide the guilt of a person when they had many unanswered questions? How did they know a man spoke the truth when he said "It was an accident" and the other person had died?

Suppose two people had a boundary dispute on adjoining property. In ancient times, they placed a stone to mark the lines. In fact, there are injunctions in Proverbs against moving such markers—which would be like stealing land from the neighbor. Suppose two honest, upright people disputed the boundary. One said the rock had been moved and the other man, who denied it, appeared to be telling the truth also.

Even today, we have this happen. My friend Linda wanted her church to hire her as a Christian educator. One elder was all for it, but a second elder took the position that Linda ought to devote her time without charge. "It's a gift God has given her." Who was correct?

When honest differences arise in the church, in business, in the neighborhood, how do we resolve them? We can go into friendly arbitration, hire lawyers, or talk until we reach a middle ground or one side prevails over the other. Or we could take the simple approach that ancient Israelites took—casting the lot. It may not be quite as primitive as it sounds. And it may be a lot more significant than gambling, which is built around taking chances.

But first, what does the Bible say about "casting the lot"? To the surprise of many, there are a number of instances of that very act, such as:

- Dividing the land among the twelve tribes when they entered the Promised Land (Numbers 26:55)
- Selecting Achan as the thief (Joshua 7:16–20)
- Picking out Jonathan as the soldier who had eaten during a fast (1 Samuel 14:42)
- Correctly pointing to Jonah as the one who had offended God (Jonah 1:7)

Let's look at the last mention of casting of lots in the Bible, found in Acts 1:12–26. After Judas's betrayal of Jesus and his suicide, the apostles met together to choose his successor. They studied the qualifications and narrowed it down to two candidates, Joseph and Matthias. They used the casting of lots to decide. But it was more than a quick exhortation "Draw a straw."

"Then they prayed and said, 'Lord, you know everyone's heart. Show us which one of these two you have chosen to take the place in this ministry . . .' And they cast lots for them, and the lot fell on Matthias . . ." (vv. 24–26).

They prayed—but it was more than going through the ritual of asking. In their thinking, God had already made a choice. Their role was to "hear" that choice. "Show us which one of these two you have chosen." This, then, wasn't random gambling or taking a chance, but it was serious business. When they cast the lot—and we're never told anywhere in the Bible precisely how they did that—they trusted that God would guide their selection and they would learn the will of God by the result.

That's drastic thinking and behavior. It really speaks of trust, commitment, and a willingness to lay everything in divine hands. So maybe the practice isn't so archaic after all. The methods aren't what we use, but the intention comes out the same: "Show us your will." And somehow God has many ways to make that will known.

I'm not urging people to rush out and draw lots, but I suggest we think of the issue *behind* the lot. The people of God truly believed that God had selected the answer and they had to open themselves to find it. In that time, they chose the lot as their means of discerning God's direction. In our culture and in our day, we try other methods. They drew lots as an act of faith, and in their hearts, they trusted that whatever answer came up, it would be exactly what God wanted. Perhaps, then, we need to focus on what God wants instead of how we discern that will.

"I figure that if God wants me to do something and I pray for guidance—sincerely ask," my friend Bill said recently, "then I believe God will show me."

"Exactly right," I said. "You believe, isn't that so?"

"Of course, I do."
I smiled. "So did they."
And for me, that's the secret behind casting lots.

Modern Proverb: *When we sincerely want to know the right decision, we can trust God to show us.*

Who's Right?

*The one who first states a case seems right, until the
other comes and cross-examines.*

Proverbs 18:17

In the 1970s, Anne Dunivin and I represented our local church
at a special meeting of our denomination when we were making important decisions about the role of women in ministry.
Our presbytery had it set up so that one spoke for giving
women full rights for five minutes and the next one spoke
against it for the same length of time.

After perhaps half an hour of the back-and-forth speaking,
Anne turned to me and whispered, "Whenever anyone speaks,
I agree with that person, and then the next one speaks and I
agree with that argument."

I smiled because I had much the same reaction. Part of our
dilemma then—and in many situations today—is that most of
us tend to believe that although there may be many sides to
every story, only one is fully accurate. Yet if we watch and
believe TV ads for cosmetics, cars, paper towels, or soaps,
companies try to tell us their product is superior. Within minutes we see a commercial for a competitive product and we're
no longer sure. Can all of them be superior?

The point of this proverb is that we need to listen to both
sides before we decide which is right. This approach was especially important in meting out justice in matters of the law. It's
easy for the words or the emotions to cloud our judgment. We
have known of innocent people being convicted of crimes without being able to present their story or to prove their innocence.

But this proverb has another aspect worth considering. It
has to do with giving others an even break. Too often we take

a position or an opinion, and we're convinced it's not only correct, but that any other position must, by nature, be wrong. Consequently, we'll do whatever it takes to make our position prevail. We get so anxious to place our cause in a strong light that, perhaps unconsciously, we cast a shadow of doubt over those who disagree. Or we overlook significant and important aspects of their positions.

Consequently, if we present our cause first, it seems right and we may convince those who listen. But when the other side gets a chance to speak, the arguments begin to cast doubt on our position. That's how our legal system works. It's also how differences work in human relationships.

Imagine when someone takes a strong stand and an adversary points out the other's errors of judgment or (worse yet) behavior. In this case, the new presentation brings shame and humiliation.

I remember once that a newly married couple, both with low-income jobs, rented a house from someone I knew well. After four months, the owner evicted them. The couple complained to me about the landlord's terrible treatment of them, his refusal to make repairs, and his unwillingness to talk things over with them. I felt rage growing inside me, although I didn't understand how this could be so. I had always thought the owner was an honorable man, and I wondered how he could be so cruel and heartless.

Could this really be so? I pondered, and yet the couple's story sounded so convincing.

Finally, I called the owner and asked about them.

"Oh, since you've listened to them, let me come over and tell you my side of it," he suggested. I agreed, and within minutes, he was there. In their presence, he said that they had never paid a full month's rent and that he had given them the apartment at a greatly reduced rate because the husband agreed that he would do some needed repairs. The young man did install a new toilet, which the owner provided. But he didn't do anything else.

The couple denied and disputed everything the owner said. Soon it became a matter of accusations and angry words. I asked them to stop. Once I heard both sides of the story, I saw things a lot more clearly. (A few days later, I learned that the couple rarely stayed in an apartment longer than six months because they wouldn't pay their rent.)

I had silently condemned that landlord, based on what the young couple said. Had I not investigated further, I could have done the owner a grave injustice.

This proverb urges us to hear everything before we make decisions. It's too easy to believe the first one who speaks, especially if that person is loud, eloquent, or convincing.

Someone has said, "The prosecutor's case is always right—until the defendant's case has been presented." It's the old idea that the first seems right. And that means a bad cause can be made to seem right.

This proverb is not only for judges, but for all of us. We must sift the evidence and avoid believing the first report about anything. We need to consider, accept advice, and guard against our own prejudice. We still may never know who is right, but we'll at least make our mistakes honorably.

Modern Proverb: *Don't listen only to those who speak first and present a good case. Get the whole story before making a decision.*

Weighing Falsely

A false balance is an abomination to the Lord, but an accurate weight is his delight.

Proverbs 11:1

Diverse weights and diverse measures are both alike an abomination to the Lord.

Proverbs 20:10

Four days after I first moved to a rural area of Kenya, I went to the nearest town to buy supplies for a girls' dormitory where my wife had just become headmistress. The "town" consisted of one wide street, one block long, with small *dukas* (stores) built like row houses. At the time, all of the merchants were East Indians. Except for the *duka* at the very end with a gasoline pump, most of the merchants carried essentially the same products. Their prices varied slightly from product to product.

Being a practical person, I went to the shop where they sold gasoline and decided to buy the other things we needed, such as corn, beans, rice, flour, tea, and sugar. The owner treated me courteously and even offered me a cup of tea while his African helper filled my order.

Because I was buying for a girls' dormitory, that meant a lot of profit if he got our business. On the first day, however, the trader lost my business. As I sat there, waiting for his helper to bring out the *gunias* (one-hundred-pound burlap bags) of beans, the owner waited on African customers. Most of the Africans were poor and bought small amounts of tea, sugar, and other items. The merchant had a supply of weights and laid them on the balance scale.

Then I saw how he operated his scales. Sometimes Africans came into the *duka* to sell him products, such as raw honey or ground nuts (peanuts). For them, he used a second set of weights, which he kept hidden behind the counter—one set of weights to buy, and a different set to sell. Fortunately for me,

219

everything I bought came in such large quantities that they had been pre-measured before reaching his place of business.

Such a practice shocked me, and I told one of the Africans about it later. "Yes, I know about him, and so does everyone else," the African said. "There is nothing you can do if you trade with him."

"Then why does anyone go there?"

"He gives credit. Most of the others do not."

That was my first experience with dishonest weights, and it made me think of ancient Israel. What a problem it must have been to measure goods bought and sold in ancient times. Supposedly, the scales were based on the principle of balancing against a standard stone weight. Which meant that grains or gold could be weighed fairly only if the stone weights were accurate. Some merchants had two sets of weights. When buying barley, they used heavy weights, and that enabled them to get more of the grain for the prices they paid. When they sold the same barley, they used the lighter weights to increase their profits.

From the days of the Law of Moses forward, God has spoken against such dishonesty. The reasons are obvious. No one wants to be cheated or taken advantage of. And merchants who cheated the poor committed the worst abuses. That hasn't changed very much.

Today, however, weights have become standardized. We can know the net weight of anything we buy because the law requires the manufacturers to print it on the label. And yet, despite the standardization, those labels and containers may be deceptive. For instance, I've noticed cans of ground coffee in the grocery stores. Most of them are one-pound cans—sixteen ounces. However, a few of them are the same sized cans, but when we read the label, we discover they contain only twelve ounces. That's not dishonest, but it seems deceptive.

Aside from issues like that, most of us assume we have no problem keeping the law of weights and measures. We might even pride ourselves on it. Yet maybe we need to take another look at this. Maybe it helps if we ask, *Why did Yahweh give the people such laws?*

"To treat everyone the same" sounds like a good answer, and it surely is. And to treat everyone the same means that when we buy a two-liter bottle, we can assume it contains exactly that amount. We don't want to cheat and we don't want to be cheated.

The whole concept really hones in on the principle of honesty. We don't want to be cheated, so we don't cheat. The problem is that we tend to be a bit selective in the way we deal with honest weights.

Here's one example. Bonnie works for a large corporation on a computer terminal. Her employers pay for seven hours of work and give her one hour for a lunch break. Bonnie is always there on time to begin and she stays until quitting time. So far, so good.

What Bonnie doesn't think about is that she uses her computer to send and receive personal e-mail messages on her employer's time. When my wife was going to have surgery, Bonnie asked me to e-mail her as soon as Shirley was in recovery (she knew I'd have my laptop with me).

"But you'll be at work," I said. "Do they allow that?"

"Not really," she said, "but everybody does it. Gets boring otherwise, just sitting in front of that screen all day."

I didn't send Bonnie an e-mail, because I decided that by doing so, I'd contribute to her stealing time from her employer. True, Bonnie didn't "steal" as we think of it, but the principle is the same, isn't it? An honest weight also implies honesty when reporting time or work hours.

I also knew a man, then an airline office manager, who was a partner in a real estate company. Apparently, he spent about ten hours every week handling real estate business while on his airline job. Once he left two hours early to show a house to a client. The company eventually fired the man.

I've often wondered how people like the former airline executive or Bonnie would feel if their employers deducted pay for the time they spent on personal things? I'm sure they would rush to the front of the protest line.

So what do we do? How do we handle such situations? My response is that it calls for serious—very serious—heart searching. Should employers, unknowingly, pay for the time we spend doing personal, non-business-related tasks? I'll put it another way: If I am going to live the life that pleases Yahweh, that means it's a life of constant self-examination. Part of that examination involves what we often call the golden rule. That is, we treat others the way we want to be treated.

If I were the employer, would it please me for my employees to spend their work time doing personal business? It's worth thinking about.

Modern Proverb: *Cheating anyone in any form displeases God.*

A Little Honesty

> *Honest balances and scales are the LORD's; all the weights in the bag are his work.*
>
> Proverbs 16:11

In some ways, it sounds strange that God put so much emphasis on little things, such as weights and measures. Of course, measures need to be honest and reliable—that's obvious. But it amazes me that God linked concerns over honest measures with being Yahweh, the One who brought the people out of slavery.

It was while I was thinking about weights and measures that I saw this for the first time in Leviticus 19:35–36: "You shall not cheat in measuring length, weight, or quantity. You shall have honest balances, honest weights, an honest ephah, and an honest hin: I am the LORD your God, who brought you out of the land of Egypt."

And it's not just in that passage. Not only did the Law of Moses speak against dishonest trade practices, but the Old Testament prophets—such as Ezekiel, Amos, and Micah—often raised their voices in protest as well. Whether scales or plumb lines, they spoke about the matter of honesty.

Weights were usually made of stone, with each weight inscribed and all kept together in a bag. The basic unit of weight in daily use was the shekel, which weighed about eleven grams. The ephah referred to dry measure and was used for grains. It was the equivalent to the capacity of a container large enough to hold a man and was reckoned as one-tenth of the load of a donkey. In those days, despite all the attempts at standard measurement, the weights varied from city to city. That couldn't be helped.

This proverb is saying something much more important: False weights—deliberately dishonest units of measure—were an *abomination*. The word *abomination* is about as strong as language gets—it's almost like a divine curse. Then the sages further stated that accurate scales and weights belong to God. They stressed that God laid down how much weight should be in a shekel or the capacity of an ephah. They also implied that God watched when deception went on. Such proverbs tried to press home the lesson that God expects scrupulous honesty.

Teachers of the Law took this idea so seriously that they laid down strict rules to prevent even unintentional dishonesty. For example, they said that shopkeepers had to wipe the measures at least twice a week, the weights once a week, and the scales after every weighing.

Those leaders also laid down strict rules about the actual weighing and measuring procedure. For instance, they couldn't measure land in winter and then again in summer, because the measuring line shrinks in summer. They couldn't keep their weights in salt because brine made them heavier.

We may laugh at the meticulousness of such rules, but perhaps they grasped something many of us don't consider. I thought of a saying I used to hear as a child: "Honesty in little things isn't a little thing."

They're such little things, and yet it's in the little things that we miss God more than most of us acknowledge. We wouldn't think of robbing a bank, but what if a cashier gives us an extra ten dollars? Or even fifty cents too much change? Then what?

"Not worth bothering about" is the answer I've commonly heard. Or here's the other one: "They're set up to make allowances for those small mistakes." Those are the ways we justify our behavior and push away the little things that seem so irrelevant to the total picture of life. But I wonder.

How little are the little things?

When Shirley and I were dating, we had a little joke going with a number of our friends, based on the story of Lot fleeing Sodom. In Genesis 19, divine messengers told Lot they would destroy the city of Sodom. They urged him to take his family and flee to the hills.

A reluctant Lot said, ". . . I cannot flee to the hills, for fear the disaster will overtake me and I die. Look, that city is near enough to flee to, and it is a little one. Let me escape there— is it not a little one?—and my life will be saved!" (Genesis 19:19–20).

Although the messengers agreed that he could go to the little town of Zoar, he went that far only because he was told to get out or die.

From that story, we picked up the saying "It's only a little city. Is it not a little one?" We used to tease each other with those words whenever we faced small issues in life. For example, one time I gave my good friend John Burbank three pages I had typed and paper-clipped together.

He recognized it as paper from my office. "Oh, is that not a little city?" he asked.

Embarrassment swept over me. I could have used all the standard answers: "Oh, they'll never miss it" or "Who will know?" But it forced me to realize that I had done something dishonest. True, it was a tiny city!

Another Old Testament story involves King Saul. Before battling the Amalekites, God had told him to destroy every person, including the animals. Saul won the victory, and when Samuel, God's prophet, came to visit him, Saul said, "May you be blessed by the LORD; I have carried out the command of the LORD" (1 Samuel 15:13).

Saul hadn't done what God told him—he had spared the life of King Agag and kept the animals alive. Doesn't that seem like such a little thing? I mean, what are a few animals anyway? Okay, he should have killed King Agag, but why make such a big thing over it?

God made a big thing over it. That "small" act of disobedience marked Saul's rejection by God. Although the man stayed in power for several more years, he no longer had God's favor.

And yet, it was such a small mistake. *Wasn't it?*

Did God really reject Saul over something minor like that? Sounds harsh to our modern minds. But if we think of the reason behind divine commands, we can get closer to the principle. The principle in the story of Saul isn't really about sacrifices or killing the enemies. Isn't it about the little acts of faithfulness? Observing the small acts of obedience?

Could it be that the real test of our relationship to God and other people rests on such little things? Is it possible that the best way to check our commitment doesn't depend on the big issues, but in the small things—the little cities?

Modern Proverb: *Honesty in everything counts—and it especially counts in the little things.*

Kings Rule

*If a king judges the poor with equity, his throne will be
established forever.*

Proverbs 29:14

When I was a teen, I loved to read novels or see films where
the king or the princess leaves the palace and, for a time, lives
the life of a commoner, such as *The Prince and the Pauper.*
One of the great moments of insight invariably comes when
the now-disguised ruler sees grave injustice done, such as
sending someone to a debtor's prison or a family being thrown
out of its home for not paying exorbitant taxes.

What made those escapes of film or books pleasurable is
that the ruler always returned a changed person and instituted
reforms. Ah, if only life always imitated fiction.

Reality challenges such stories. The role of rulers has
always been a problem for humanity. Nations need leadership,
and that's rather obvious. Although we may argue over the
form it takes, we recognize that we need those with power to
take up the cause of the powerless. Nowadays, few countries
still have kings, but the principles stated in Proverbs work just
as well. It's really not about the king as a person or an office,
but about justice and equity.

Isn't it amazing to see the link between the ruler and the
poor? The way the judicial system treats the poor accurately
indicates the quality of justice in a country. The poor are the
most likely to suffer from judicial discrimination, because they
have no one to defend them. True justice treats rich and poor
alike and favors neither.

The idea that justice with fairness and equity builds loyalty
and respect that protect and keep governments strong is part of

what this proverb is saying: "If a king [or the system of justice] judges the poor with equity, his throne will be established forever."

For the sages of Israel, good kings idealized the qualities of the nation. The people expected their rulers to handle matters with integrity and, above all, justice. We see glimpses of this during the reign of David and Solomon.

1 Kings 3:16–28, for example, tells of Solomon settling a dispute between two prostitutes over a baby, as I tell elsewhere. The story concludes, "All Israel heard of the judgment that the king had rendered; and they stood in awe of the king, because they perceived that the wisdom of God was in him, to execute justice" (v. 28).

Proverbs 20:8 says, "A king who sits on the throne of judgment winnows all evil with his eyes." We don't know, but there are some scholars who insist that the king sat on a special throne where he decided on significant cases. According to 1 Kings 7:7, Solomon had a special Hall of the Throne "where he was to pronounce judgment, the Hall of Justice . . ."

Normally, most cases were heard from elders in the local courts, and they usually held them at the gates of the cities. Apparently, Israelites had the right to appeal and to bring their grievance directly to the king. His answer would be the final appeal.

Every king wasn't a wise and brilliant Solomon, so what could people reasonably expect from their rulers?

First, they could expect that all wrongdoers would be brought to trial and punished for their deeds. Kings, being among the best educated and surrounded by a counsel of advisers, were assumed to have the discernment to see through schemes of evil. Subjects in the kingdom expected them to separate truth from falsehood as winnowers separated chaff from wheat (see Proverbs 20:8). They were to punish them as crushingly as the wheel of a cart pulverized the sheaves when it was driven back and forth across the threshing floor.

Second, the king was to see to it that the rights of the poor and the needy were protected from the sharp practices and flagrant injustices of the rich and powerful. More than anything else, the common people yearned for this quality so they could live in peace.

Unfortunately, that was also the quality most of the kings lacked. Ahab is a glaring example of a king who not only looked away from injustice, but actively encouraged it by his own example of allowing an innocent to be accused, convicted, and killed because the king wanted the land.

Throughout the Old Testament, some of the prophets' harshest words strike at kings and political leaders for using their power to further their own ends, especially at the expense of the poor, who should have been the object of special care. Here's one example: "The LORD rises to argue his case; he stands to judge the peoples. The LORD enters into judgment with the elders and princes of his people: It is you who have devoured the vineyard; the spoil of the poor is in your houses. What do you mean by crushing my people, by grinding the face of the poor? . . ." (Isaiah 3:13–15).

The test of leaders' power was the extent to which they kept faith with those who put the least amount of pressure on them. Although that seems obvious, what most of us don't consider is that those in need are not only the responsibility of those in possession of power but our responsibility as well.

No place in the New Testament does it say this more clearly than in James 1:27: "Religion that is pure and undefiled before God, the Father, is this: to care for orphans and widows in their distress, and to keep oneself unstained by the world."

In that simple statement we have the principle—and our obligation—laid out for us. We are to care for our own relationship with God, but we also have to provide for others who cannot care for themselves. In fact, I see no way that we can separate the two.

There are many ways to oppress the needy, and probably the most obvious is to ignore their needs. We do it with an air of self-righteousness by exclaiming, "If they'd only get out and work the way I do." Or we label them as lazy and stupid—especially if we can convince ourselves that they really do like to live in poverty and inferior housing.

When I first came into the Christian faith, I didn't hear

much about concern for the poor. For us, *poor* and *hungry* represented Africa and India. We were all white and middle class, and most of the people we associated with had the same values and outlook that we did.

The late 1960s did more to awaken me than anything else. So far as I can recall, that's when I began hearing words such as *disenfranchised.* A few courageous leaders dared to point out poverty and injustice. I didn't like it—and even more I didn't like that those pointed fingers were aimed at me and people just like me.

I cooperated and slowly opened my arms to wrap around those "less fortunate ones" (and I suspect at times my tone was that condescending).

One day in 1984, when I studied the small letter of 1 John, the power of the message grabbed me and wouldn't let me run away from it. John wrote, "We know love by this, that he [Jesus] laid down his life for us—and we ought to lay down our lives for one another" (1 John 3:16). I'd heard that for years and it often gave me a warm feeling of how Christians reach out and care for one another.

But that day in 1984—and I think for the first time in my life—I connected it with the next two verses: "How does God's love abide in anyone who has the world's goods and sees a brother or sister in need and yet refuses help? Little children, let us love, not in word or speech, but in truth and action" (vv. 17–18).

I hadn't done much caring for those who were poor. Our church had a Good Samaritan Fund that we used to help poor people pay rent or buy food, as well as a food pantry. But that seemed so cold and distant.

A number of Christians I know began to move into the areas where the poor and needy lived. We saw that we had worldly goods and they didn't. Some supported night shelters for the homeless, worked in soup kitchens, and built homes for the poor.

For two years, Shirley and I worked with an organization called AID Atlanta—we worked with people with AIDS at a time when many Christians looked down on them. "They're the lepers of today," Shirley said. "They're the needy and they need people like us."

She had had nurses' training and worked with the near-dying—bathing, shaving, and washing their clothes—and was often at their bedside when they left this life. I worked with men who wanted a friend, someone to talk to and occasionally take them out to eat.

In some ways, our actions seem small, almost insignificant, but we tried to look at the biblical statement to open ourselves to those in need because we had goods. We gave.

Maybe that's the area of struggle for all of us. Could it be that by shutting our eyes and closing our hearts, we're actually oppressing the poor?

Modern Proverb: *To care for the poor and to uphold their cause is the mark of true justice. And justice makes nations endure.*